HANDFASTED
and
HEARTJOINED

Rituals for Uniting a Couple's Hearts and Lives

LADY MAEVE RHEA

CITADEL PRESS
Kensington Publishing Corp.
www.kensingtonbooks.com

CITADEL PRESS books are published by

Kensington Publishing Corp.
850 Third Avenue
New York, NY 10022

All Kensington titles, imprints, and distributed lines are available at special quantity discounts for bulk purchases for sales promotions, premiums, fund-raising, educational, or institutional use. Special book excerpts or customized printings can also be created to fit specific needs. For details, write or phone the office of the Kensington special sales manager: Kensington Publishing Corp., 850 Third Avenue, New York, NY 10022, attn: Special Sales Department, phone 1-800-221-2647.

Citadel Press and the Citadel logo are trademarks of Kensington Publishing Corp.

First printing May 2001

10 9 8 7 6 5 4 3 2 1

Printed in the United States of America

ISBN 0-8065-2194-5

Cataloging data may be obtained from the Library of Congress.

This book is dedicated to all the wonderful people who have let me be a part of their special day: Kathy and Jim, Maddie and Nate, Chris and Kristy, Frank and Christina, Mary and Pete, Carole and Mike, Nan and Shari, Walter and Pat, Kathleen and Bill, Bruce and Kat, Tony and Diane, Lee and Ray, Nicki and Collin, Liz and Joe, Celeste and Bob, Robert and Alicyn, Henry and Laura, Brenda and Tyler, Kim and Joseph, Karen and Tom, Amanda and Steven, Karli and Stan, and those of you who don't wish to have your names listed.

Thanks for the memories.

HANDFASTED
and
HEARTJOINED

CONTENTS

PREFACE

October 1996

The maid of honor steps forward, a branch of willow in her hands. With grace and dignity, she touches the woman standing in front of her on the forehead, on the lips, and on the chest. Then, she touches the man who stands next to the woman on the forehead, on the lips, and on the chest.

As she does so she says clearly and with power: "My gift is the gift of the Mother. It is the strength of the willow wand, a strength that will bend where others might break. It is the strength to seek conciliation in the heat of anger. A gift of compromise, of giving while in the grip of selfishness."

She turns and hands the willow wand to the facilitating priest, who places it on the decorated altar where it joins other simple yet powerful symbols of the magickal rite that is taking place: the Rite of Handfasting.

This is the scene that runs through my mind while the young woman sitting on my sofa wipes her teary, red eyes and nose and sniffles dramatically.

"Let's go over this again, Ramona.* Just why do you want to have a handfasting?" I ask gently with a smile. I am seeking to reveal the truth that this young woman is hiding from.

Also seated on the sofa (but as far from Ramona as he can be and still be on the same piece of furniture) is a stony-faced young man, arms crossed, the belligerent sneer on his mouth just barely concealed by his underlying desire not to hurt her.

"Well, I am a Witch . . ."

"Ramona, are you a Witch, or are you a Wiccan? There is a difference, and it will make a difference in your ceremony." Again I attempt to get to the root of the problem.

"I guess I'm a Wiccan . . . I mean, I'm a solitary and I've never been initiated . . . why, does that make a difference?"

"Yes. Everything makes a difference when we are discussing a Rite of Handfasting."

I turn to the young man and smile. "How do you feel about getting handfasted instead of being married in the traditional way, Tony?" I pour him another cup of tea and wait to hear his answer.

He says what he thinks Ramona expects him to say. "Yeah—I guess. It's okay with me if it's okay with her. Whatever she wants."

I sip my tea and consider how I am going to tell these well-meaning young people that I cannot in good conscience facilitate their handfasting.

I take a deep breath and plunge in: "There are numerous ceremonies that fall under the title of *handfasting*. And I am sure that at least one of them is appropriate for the two of you, but here is my concern: I do not *marry* anyone. No one can perform a binding ceremony that is spiritually valid except the

---

*All names have been changed.

two people involved. In other words, I can facilitate your ceremony. I can help you write your vows, I can guide you through the intricacies of the different aspects of the different sorts of rituals, but the only person who can marry you is . . . you.

"And that means you must be very clear on why you are getting married; what you want from the marriage and what you want from the ceremony. From our conversation and the notes I've taken for the past two hours, it's obvious that you are not yet clear on what you want or why. I am going to suggest that you do some meditating, both together. . . ." Tony struggles to suppress a smirk, ". . . and by yourselves. When you have some unconfused answers and sound motivations, give me a call and we'll talk again."

Ramona is not happy with this, but Tony lets out a breath of repressed anxiety. He is more than delighted to leave with no plans having been made.

Weeks pass and neither Tony nor Ramona call me, but then I had not expected that they would.

A few months later, I happen to meet Ramona on the street. She looks more miserable that when I last saw her, if that is possible. We stop to have coffee together and I ask about Tony.

She blinks back some tears. "Tony dumped me. He said all the witchy stuff was just too crazy."

I take a deep breath. "I could tell that he felt that way when we were talking at my house. Do you understand now why I wanted you to do some more thinking about getting handfasted? Handfasting isn't just a big party preceded by somebody mumbling some outdated words over the couple getting married. It is a powerful magickal ritual that changes the lives of everyone who takes part. There was no way I could commit myself to assisting you in having a handfasting when it was clear that Tony wasn't going to participate willingly, much less wholeheartedly."

Ramona and I talk a little more and then we part. I know that she will continue to seek out "Tonys" until she finally decides she no longer wants to star in her particular soap opera, and I also know that she thinks that I just don't understand.

But I do understand. And that is why I am writing this book: to assist the many Pagans, Wiccans, and Witches who want to have their Rite of Handfasting be one of the most powerful and significant things in their lives—without alienating all their friends and relatives, and without going bankrupt.

HANDFASTED
and
HEARTJOINED

1

WHY GET HANDFASTED?

The question above is, in my opinion, the most essential question that people who are considering such a ritual ask themselves. And the answer should go beyond "Because we're in love."

Handfasting and marriage rituals go back as far as humans do. People have a deep need to mark with rite and celebration the formation of new family units. But the reasons people got married in ancient times—and indeed in the not-so-distant past—were very different from the reasons that people get married today. There are many societies today that do not share our Western romantic notions and their reasons for marriage are still quite dissimilar from ours.

Our modern society has moved beyond many of the reasons our ancestors had for marriage. Unlike a hundred years ago, these days a single person can actually take care of herself by herself. In our society, we no longer need social approval to engage in sexual behavior or to live together. Most people no longer believe that women need to be controlled or suppressed; they no longer need to be the property of a man. In addition, while the pressure to have children (ready or not) may still exist, there is no longer the monstrous social or religious condemnation of those who have children out of wedlock (which is an interesting word, if you think about it). Further, these days it is generally accepted by society that romantic companionship does not need to be legalized by a religious ritual. We are no longer ruled by those things. Nowadays, we are ruled by our needs and by our desires.

While I will not go into detail about the manifold reasons for marriage in times past and in other societies, I will assert that "being in love" rarely factored into it. And contrary to the premise of most romance novels, the unwilling bride being married to a man she didn't even know was a fairly common occurrence. Nor was it uncommon for a man to be married to a woman he'd never met. Yet they were expected to abide together and contribute to the commonweal without too much protest. It did not matter whether they loved each other or not.

Romantic love as the basis for a union is a recent notion and is almost totally confined to Western European culture. In some societies (such as the Brahminate societies of India), romantic love was (and is) viewed as a sickness, or as a moral weakness. Some societies consider infatuation to be a form of insanity. (In fact, the Yanomamo believe that romantic love is a demon and the experience of the emotion must be beaten to drive it out!)

Indeed, romantic love alone is one of the great reasons why many marriages *don't* work. By itself, it is not, in my opinion, a good reason to get married.

Romantic love is a good reason to give cards, flowers, and candy; an excellent reason to experience great sex and ecstatic sensuality, but it is *not* a good reason to get married. A marriage based solely on romantic love is going to have problems.

The major problem with romantic love is it doesn't last—at least not without a great deal of commitment and work. That initial "rush" wears off rather rapidly, eroded by the day-to-day conflicts that any set of people living in close proximity will experience. Thus, if romantic love is the sole basis for a marriage, that marriage will fail. And this is true for any coupling, heterosexual, homosexual, polygamous, or monogamous.*

Many of the old reasons for getting married are gone—and I say good riddance. But what are good reasons for getting handfasted?

I can only think of one: to create a stable, functional, nurturing, healthy, family unit that will provide room for *all* of its members (including children), so that those members are able to achieve their fullest physical, emotional, and psychic potential.

Creating such a unit requires friendship and a sense of humor; self-confidence and a commitment to growth; autonomy for all members of the union; a sound economic foundation; honesty, trust and reliability; and shared common interests. When you put all those factors together, you get what I consider to be true love. An additional requirement for

---

*For the sake of simplicity I refer to the people involved in a relationship as "the couple" although my intention is to include all types of unions.

Pagans, Wiccans, and Witches* is that the couple have a shared religious philosophy.

Pagans must consider the last requirement carefully when planning to be handfasted to a non-Pagan. While there are some handfastings between Pagans and non-Pagans that do work, they are few and far between. The fundamental philosophical differences between Pagan and non-Pagan belief systems are usually too extreme and the frictions between the two are almost insurmountable.

If you are considering marrying a non-Pagan, think carefully about the concessions, diminutions, and modifications you will have to make in your life. Although it is sad to say, Pagan beliefs are not taken seriously by most members of our society. You will need to be prepared for the times when your non-Pagan, or his or her family, will scoff at, deride, and in general be intolerant of your beliefs. It's important to consider how this will affect any children that result from your union, and you must carefully weigh its spiritual costs.

The only times I have known these unions to work was when the non-Pagan was, in reality, a Pagan and simply hadn't gotten around to realizing it.

What Is a Handfasting and How Does It Differ From Traditional Wedding Ceremonies?

A handfasting is not a Pagan wedding. There are several fundamental differences that will affect how the ceremony and celebration are planned, how they are paid for, and primarily, how they will affect non-Pagan family and friends.

---

*For simplicity's sake, I will use the term Pagan to mean Pagans, Wiccans, Witches, and other polytheists.

First: *A handfasting is a magickal rite,* in which magickal energies are raised within a sacred space. Usually a Goddess-form and a God-form are invoked.* Directional guardians may be evoked and other appropriate God-forms may also be evoked or invoked by the participants. When the energies are correctly raised and manipulated by the persons involved, they are tangible and they can be energizing, stimulating, or frightening to the gathered witnesses. This is a factor with which you must deal very early on in the planning of a handfasting when non-Pagans are involved. I have seen more than one handfasting where the non-Pagans became frightened and frightened people are dangerous people.

Second: *The handfasting involves vows that are created by the people who are joining their lives;* vows that are pertinent to *their* concerns and interests. It is essential that the couple write their own vows; however, they will often need assistance from a facilitator who is levelheaded and is not emotionally involved in the union.

Third: *A handfasting has a mutually agreed-upon duration of the union.* Any sensible facilitator will make sure that the time period the couple agrees upon is realistic.

It is the duty of the facilitator to remember that all promises made within a sacred ritual space and called into manifestation by the magick of the persons involved must be able to be kept. "Until death do us part" is not a keepable vow. *No one* knows what will happen ten, thirty, or fifty years from now. Although the couple may have much in common in the beginning of their relationship, people grow and change. They may find they no longer have anything in common after a span of years. They may find that the person they love madly today is no

---

*For certain types of homosexual handfastings only one gender will be invoked.

longer even on their list of friends in a decade or two. At that point the handfasting and heartjoining is over. The couple separates or divorces. If that should occur and if a promise to stay together until death, or eternity, or "as long as the stars shall shine" has been made during the magickal Rite of Handfasting, real magickal disaster will occur.

When a couple is in the grip of the romantic love that so often begins a relationship, the reality of what I've just mentioned is often overlooked. Of all the duties of the facilitator, assisting the couple in writing their vows and in helping them set a duration for the union is the most important.

Fourth: *The only persons authorized to handfast or marry anybody are the couple themselves.* Perhaps the most significantly different aspect of a handfasting as opposed to traditional Western weddings is that Pagans believe that no outside person, religious institution, or secular power has the ability to marry anyone.* Pagans believe that the magickal act of handfasting is effective **only** when performed by the couple directly involved. To pretend otherwise—to assert that a minister or secular authority can pronounce anybody to be anything—is analogous to saying that when a midwife exclaims "It's a girl!" she has just created the gender of the child. She hasn't; she has simply announced the fact.

Therefore, when a priest or priestess presents the handfasted couple to the assembled witnesses, she or he does not say "I pronounce you man and wife," she or he merely announces— in a ceremonial manner—that the couple is now handfasted and heartjoined.

If you consider the above, you must also consider that many states' marital laws violate the constitutional rights of Pagans

---

*The Society of Friends and some "primitive" Christian religions also practice "self-marriage."

by requiring the Pagan couple to participate in ceremonies that are counter to their religious beliefs in order to make their relationships legal. Someday, someone with enough money and time will challenge those codes but for now, you must know that in many states, in order to have a legally recognized union, you will have to hold a civil ceremony as well as a religious one. Yes, this is terribly unfair, religiously and spiritually polluting, and discriminates against Paganism in favor of other religions. But for now, that is the way it is. (To find out if you live in such a state, see Appendix I.)

2

FIRST
CONSIDERATIONS

When a traditional couple has made the decision to marry, the first thing they usually do is find out which dates are available at their desired reception hall. Almost everything else can be arranged around that: the date of the ceremony, when to order the invitations, what kind of a wedding dress to purchase, and so on. If they are having a religious ceremony, they may have a few choices to make but the type or level of ceremony that they will have is seldom a consideration. For most, that decision was made long ago by the dicta of their religion.

A Pagan couple, on the other hand, has to first decide what type of handfasting they desire and what level is appropriate to their needs. After that and other important spiritual decisions have been made, I usually advise them to rush and find out what days are available at the reception site of their choice.

First, they must decide if they are going to have a Simple Handfasting; a High Rite of Handfasting; or—if they are both Witches—a magickal ritual called the Rite of Becoming One.

Simple Handfasting

A Simple Handfasting is the rite usually chosen by a couple who want to "try on" a socially supported union without applying for a legal marriage license and who do not desire the binding of intense magickal energies that can do so much damage if carelessly disregarded. It is an effective way for a couple to make their intentions clear to the community around them and to enlist the support of that community in helping the relationship grow and endure. It usually does not require a great deal of money or time, and can be done with only a few Pagan friends as witnesses.

A Simple Handfasting may also be chosen by a couple who may have had a traditional wedding years ago and now desire the religious and spiritual ceremony. However, if the couple that has had a traditional wedding chooses to then have any type of handfasting ceremony, because of the contradictory intent and energies used in a traditional wedding ceremony, a type of cleansing ritual must be performed prior to the handfasting.

A Simple Handfasting always specifies a length of time that the union will last (traditionally a year and a day), and this is woven directly into the fabric of the ceremony. The couple agrees on the length of the period and they agree to abide together for that space of time. The magickal energy of the ceremony is structured so that little psychic or spiritual damage is done if the couple separates before the agreed-upon time period is up.

High Rite of Handfasting

A couple that has carefully considered the ramifications of a magickal as well as a material union usually decides on a High Rite of Handfasting. This usually involves a legal ceremony, a considerable outlay of time, energy, money, and a great deal of involvement by other parties, including family members. While this ritual is usually done when both people are Pagans, it can be performed when one of the couple is a non-Pagan, but only after careful preparation and meditation.

A High Rite of Handfasting includes a legal ceremony and magickal binding energies that are put in place by the common consent of all involved—including the facilitating priestess and priest, the attendants, and most importantly the couple themselves.

Though this ritual is often referred to as a Pagan Wedding, the terms *wedding* or *matrimony* do not apply to this type of union. The couple is coming together as equals, as entities belonging solely to themselves, so there is no giving away of the bride, nor are there promises of obedience and submission in any of the rites of handfasting.

The magickal energies invoked by the participants in a High Rite of Handfasting will enable the couple to sustain their union for the length of the handfasting contract. As I wrote earlier, that contract is *never* "until death do us part," "until the end of time," or "until eternity ends." None but the gods can keep such a promise. And promises that are impossible to keep must *never* be made within a magickal space: The damage that occurs when they are broken is simply too shattering and too severe.

An acceptable length for a handfasting contract is "For as long as the love shall last." Along with this concept, the magickal intention to preserve and enhance the love so that it shall last a very long time is also woven into the ceremony. This love is not only the romantic love and sexual attraction that first bring a couple together but also the mutual respect and friendship that evolves into true love.

The Rite of Becoming One

For a couple that consists of two initiated Witches (and I do not include self-initiated in this definition), there is a very solemn magickal rite called the Rite of Becoming One. This is an intense ritual in which the couple join not only their physical and emotional selves, but also join their magickal wraiths.

This ritual requires a year of preparation and a considerable outlay of time and energy, but does not necessarily require a great deal of money, and the rewards more than compensate for the investments.

This ceremony can occur within the context of the High Rite of Handfasting, or it can also be performed as a separate ritual following the High Rite.

Now that I've described the three rituals of handfasting, I would like to make it very clear that all of these rituals have been created in recent years. While a few ancient marriage customs are still known (such as jumping the broom), no ancient handfasting rituals survived the Christian persecutions.

However, these rituals are as effective—and probably more so—as anything that might have been written hundreds of years ago. I say this because modern rituals are intended to address modern concerns and realities. Ancient rituals seldom do that.

In each handfasting described here, it is the couple who are the ones actually performing the act of union. They join with each other. They can do this in fine garments or in everyday clothing, or in no clothing at all. They can perform the ritual of their choice inside or outside, with music or without, and they can have a big party afterwards or a simple sharing of cakes and wine. It all depends on the desires of the couple.

The information in the previous pages should aid you in deciding which one of the major types of handfasting rituals is the correct one for you. It is your decision to make, for although your priestess or priest can advise you, *it is your ceremony and your lives.*

Above all other considerations that one piece of advice must be remembered and held onto firmly. For there is no other occasion when well-meaning relatives and friends will desire to introduce their own needs and wants into a ceremony and celebration as with a handfasting.

Don't let them.

It's not their handfasting.

We will look at the three types of handfasting rituals and variations in depth later in this book, but for now let us turn to the discussion of practical, nonritual matters.

3

BUDGETING FOR YOUR HANDFASTING

Having decided on the type of ritual you want, you then need to address the practical aspects of the event.

Weddings and handfastings are supposed to be happy, fulfilling times but I have seen dozens of brides, grooms, and families plunged into misery while planning and preparing for the ceremony and celebration, often so deeply that they don't seem to enjoy either. Sometimes this misery is so great that afterward there are comments from the couple such as "I'm so glad that's over," or "I would never do that again."

The misery is primarily caused by the fact that people tend to have romantic illusions about weddings and therefore they do not plan realistically.

The time, money, and pain (physical, emotional, and spiritual) involved in planning a union are the three factors that if kept in balance, will insure you will have a happy time that leaves you with feelings of satisfaction and accomplishment. They are inextricably linked and yet to deal with them they must be considered separately. The time and money part are self-explanatory but the emotional element may not be. It's important to be realistic about your ability to withstand frustration, exhaustion, and mental discomfort.

Think of your outlay of time, money, and emotion like this: The more money and time you have, the less emotional trauma you'll have to deal with. On a scale of 1 to 10, most people's budgets (and that includes time and emotion, not just money) will fall somewhere in the middle.

4

TIME

Let's start by looking at your time budget—an apt term, for you will find yourself spending time as though it were money, and like money, there is never enough. One of the most valuable handfasting gifts you can give yourself is the gift of enough time.

Most handbooks on traditional weddings suggest giving yourself at least a year to plan. This is good advice to follow. I have known of handfastings that took less than six months to plan, but they were small affairs. The bigger or more elaborate your event will be, the more time you'll need in which to plan it.

One of the most primary concerns is the date of the ceremony, which may depend in many cases on where it is to be held and whether a reception is to follow. Reception halls book events months—even years—in advance. (I know of a woman who reserved a very popular site years before she even had a fiancé. She may have had her priorities backward, but she had a very elegant reception.)

Rough estimates of time budgets for handfastings are as follows: Simple handfastings can be put together in a short time. Six weeks will actually suffice if all the components are kept very simple. Even so, expect to spend a good deal of money to balance out the slim time budget.

The High Rite of Handfasting needs a minimum of six months, and a year to plan is better.

For the Rite of Becoming One, a time budget of a year is essential. The date of the ritual will depend on the phase of the moon and the season of the year, and there will be several smaller rituals leading up to the major ritual. These are held at specified times several months in advance of the rite.

Here is a sample time budget followed by a couple who were planning a High Rite of Handfasting. I was intimately involved in this handfasting, and the dates come directly from my journal. Looking at that chapter of my life, I am amazed that we got everything done on time.

January 4, 1991: C & F announce decision to be handfasted.

February 2, 1991: Ritual is held announcing the couple's intention and drawing power from their coven's wraith to support them through the next months. The decisions made based on the outcome of that ritual are that the desired date for the handfasting would be Saturday, September 19, 1991 (Mabon Hunt).

Seven months in advance: The following decisions are made, the following actions are taken, and the following rituals are held:

- The High Rite of Handfasting is decided on.
- Buffet supper with music and dancing will be held afterward.

- Menus are devised and decisions are made regarding which foods can be homemade and what would need to be catered: Hot foods catered, cold foods and desserts homemade.
- Inspection of ritual and reception sites: four days of tramping through the snow trying to imagine what a place would look like in early autumn.
- A ritual with coven and a solitary meditation are conducted to assist the couple in making the appropriate choice: The historical house with garden is chosen because of its outdoor facilities.

Six months in advance: The following decisions are made, actions are taken, and rituals are held:

- Handfasting ritual date is set.
- A deposit is sent to ceremony and celebration site.
- A small open house is held at coven High Priestess's house to talk with non-Pagan family members. After the open house, all involved sit down and reassess the situation and wonder if getting handfasted is still a good idea. The result of the reassessment is that the responsibility for the non-Pagan family members' feelings rests on the non-Pagan family members.

March 22, 1991: After the Eostara ritual, the following decisions are made and actions taken:

- Invitations to participate in the ceremony are extended to friends within the coven and to two non-Pagan friends as well. A decision is made later that the reaction of one non-Pagan friend would be too disruptive, although the other one would handle the energy of the ritual just fine.

- A private meditation to envision the handfasting clothing of the major participants in the ceremony is held.

Five months in advance: The following decisions are made, actions are taken, and rituals are held:

- The guest list is finished and a ritual is held to provide the courage to confront both sets of parents with decisions.
- Bids are taken for the sewing of handfasting costumes from three recommended seamstresses.
- Meeting with seamstress to discuss sewing of handfasting dress. After spending several hours trying to explain Pagan aspects to seamstress, the couple decides to go with a local theater group's costume maker.
- Flowers are decided on and bids are taken from three local florists.
- Contract is signed with the chosen florist.
- A ritual of commitment is held by the friends agreeing to participate in the handfasting, with two children who are to be in the handfasting are asked to practice. An assessment of their abilities is made and one child is released from her obligation.

Four months in advance: The following decisions are made, actions are taken, and rituals are held:

- On Beltaine, energy is raised for all the members of the coven.
- The couple attends a local art show to find names of artistic photographers. Four business cards are taken.
- The photographers are interviewed, and two are eliminated. The remaining to are asked to attend an open ritual on June 22. Both photographers agree—one with great enthusiasm.

- Final decisions are made regarding menu for celebration. The help of coven members in preparing food is enlisted.
- Each person agreeing to help is given a 3×5 card with the amount of each item they are going to prepare and an agreement as to who is going to furnish the materials.
- A decision is made to hire two waitpersons to assist the coven member who volunteered to run the kitchen.
- A decision is made to serve wine punch and soft drinks instead of an open bar.
- Local theater group's costumer agrees to create the hand-fasting costumes, and a contract is signed.
- Measurements are taken for the muslin mock-up.
- A day trip to Manhattan's fabric district is made and fabric for all costumes is purchased. We look at each other and say "We spent HOW much money?" Then we have a drink at the local pub to numb the pain.

Three months in advance: The following decisions are made, actions are taken, and rituals are held:

- A ritual is held to assist couple in finding funds for expected expenses.
- One of the couple announces a promotion that means more pay but longer hours.
- At the Litha celebration, the reactions of photographers to magickal energy is assessed.
- A contract with the photographer is signed.
- A ritual of commitment is held by the couple and the four Pagan musicians who have been hired to perform during the handfasting ritual.
- The shoes for the women in ceremony are ordered.
- The rings are ordered.
- The final fittings of the costumes are made.

- A small chest freezer is purchased to hold baked goods.
- Baking commences.

Two months in advance: The following decisions are made, actions are taken, and rituals are held:

- Invitations are composed and printed on couple's computers and are mailed.
- Waitpersons are hired to assist in the kitchen.
- A legal marriage license is obtained.
- The couple's vows are written with the advice of the High Priestess and High Priest of coven.
- The baking continues and dieting begins.
- A party is held by the bride's parents for all members of the ceremony.
- The couple goes on a pre-handfasting honeymoon for ten days.

One month in advance: The following decisions are made, actions are taken, and rituals are held:

- The costumes are delivered and slight alterations are made.
- There is a reconfirmation of all contracts with all suppliers. All outstanding balances are paid.
- Alternates for photographer and musicians are arranged.
- All paper and plastic ware for celebration is purchased.
- The rings are resized to fit.
- Haircuts are had by all.
- The handfasting cord is braided during private meditation.
- A rehearsal is held at the ceremony site.
- A final ritual and meditation is held to make sure that everyone is aligned with the purpose of the ceremony.

- The cake for celebration was baked and frozen (the frozen cake was decorated a few days before the handfasting).
- The bride has a root canal. (I include this because it serves to illustrate that ordinary life doesn't stop when planning a handfasting and room must be left for the daily toil and concerns.)

September 19, 1991 (the day of the handfasting): The following decisions are made, actions are taken, and rituals are held:

- The decision to go through with it is made—as is the decision not to disown parents or to murder siblings.
- High Rite of Handfasting is held.
- Celebration is held.
- Couple goes to a local hotel and soaks in hot tub.

Now, if that list—the time budget of a couple who were clear on their needs, desires, and abilities—has left you gasping for air, can you imagine what would have happened if the couple were confused and conflicted as to what they wanted? What if they had allowed the unfulfilled dreams of parents to intrude into the handfasting process? What would have occurred if the couple had not been realistic about what they could do themselves and what they needed to hire people to do? What if they had been seduced by the dog and pony show that is sold in bridal magazines? Scary, isn't it?

When you make your time budget keep this in mind: Time is your most precious resource—use it wisely.

5

THE MONSTER CALLED MONEY

After you set the date for your handfasting and have made a time budget, a money budget comes next. You won't stick to it—no one does—but at least you will have an idea of how deeply in debt you may be going. If you have been realistic about your time budget you may find ways to let time buy what money can't. And remember—if your dreams can't be bought with either money or time, then reconsider your dreams. They may be someone else's.

For the sake of everyone's sanity, do not allow yourself the pleasant fantasy that a Pagan handfasting is an inexpensive way of getting married. It isn't. Pagan handfasting ceremonies and celebrations can cost just as much as traditional weddings and receptions and, since the Pagans actually spend time and money on the *spiritual* aspect of the ceremony, they sometimes cost more.

Who Pays for a Pagan Handfasting?

Unlike traditional weddings, the bride's family is not responsible for the majority of the costs of this event.

Because of the magick involved, it is essential that the costs be shared as equally as possible by all of the people involved. A Pagan handfasting is about sharing. Since a Pagan couple will share equally in the rewards of the handfasting ritual, they should therefore equally share the costs. This is not an absolute; there are always circumstances in which one person may have greater resources than the other, but both parties should do their utmost to contribute what they can to the ceremony and the celebration.

Homemade Events

While it is possible for a Pagan couple's friends and family to combine their resources to make a celebration "just happen," a closer look behind the scenes would show the intense planning, clear and nonemotional communication, and firmly made and honorably kept commitments that go into creating the celebration.

Many Pagans do choose a homemade ceremony and celebration; the homemade quality of the ceremony and celebration are integral to their beliefs. Again, I stress that homemade is not inexpensive.

It is essential that you carefully consider the quality of a homemade item or volunteered service against that of a purchased item or hired service. If the person preparing the home-made item or providing the service does not have a certain level of expertise in that area, there is a good chance that the quality of the item or service will be disappointing. On the other hand, some volunteers can and will provide items and services that are far better than anything you can buy. Never discount or dismiss the cost of the time involved in the homemade creation or service. Remember—more time equals less stress.

In order to help you decide what you want to be handmade and what you wish to purchase from a commercial vendor, make up a comparison worksheet. A possible worksheet to make and keep handy might look something like this:

Item or Service	Homemade Cost	Purchased Cost
1. Handfasting dress:	$400 material plus 200 hours labor	$1500 plus 20 hours to shop and fit
Qualifiers	The dress can be light yellow	store-bought dresses look too commercial
2. Celebration cake	$50 materials 15 hours	$175 1 hour to choose
Qualifiers	Will taste much better Difficult to transport	Will look prettier Prepared to go

And so it goes. Every homemade item will have an extra cost that will come out of your time budget—even if someone else is doing the work, for it will take up time that could be spent some other way.

(Re cakes: Unless you've picked a very simple one, home-made handfasting cakes are extremely difficult to transport. If the person delivering it hits one pothole wrong, the cake can crack, warp, or slide off its base. Professional bakers have shock-absorbing rigs they use to transport their cakes. Consider this carefully before having someone on the other side of the county make your cake. Believe me, I learned the hard way—and royal icing is extremely difficult to get out of auto upholstery.)

Taking all that information into account, let us now look at two actual handfasting celebrations that were homemade.

In the first we will see one that worked. In the second we will see one that failed. And in both cases we will see why.

A Simple Farm Meadow Handfasting

Carole and Mike had been together for five years and they decided they wanted to be handfasted. Neither had a lot of money, but Carole was adept at sewing and cooking and Mike was eager and willing to help in whatever way he could. Most important, they kept their dreams realistic and they had a *considerable amount of free time* in which to create the handfasting of their dreams.

They asked some dear friends who were Pagan and who lived on a small farm if they could hold the ceremony there—the answer was an enthusiastic, "Of course! We'd love it!"

A date for the middle of June was set, with an understanding that if it rained, the ceremony and the celebration would be moved into the barn. To make the barn an acceptable place in which to hold a handfasting and celebration, Mike and two of his friends spent four weekends in a row clearing out the barn, fixing the roof, and reglazing quite a few windows.

While Mike was pounding in shingle nails, Carole and her friend Marti were cooking and baking, the results of which were stored in the chest freezer at the farm. Marti and another friend sewed their own bridesmaid dresses and the High Priestess of Carole's coven sewed the handfasting dress and baked the ritual cake.

Two other friends promised to provide the music with their guitars but Carole recalled just how unreliable their car was and she planned on a tape deck as a backup in case the friends developed car problems.

The day of the handfasting dawned gray and damp. Carole called me at 6 A.M. asking if I would give my approval to have a ritual fire in the barn (they had written their ceremony to include such a fire). I refused. In fact, I refused to even have lit candles in the barn. Old barns will burn like matches even in a thunderstorm and the tiniest flame can set off a ruinous blaze in no time.

But by the time everyone had gathered at the farm—except for the two guitarists whose car had broken down a hundred miles away—the sun was shining and the ritual fire was burning nicely in a fire pit that was specially dug and lined with rocks that wouldn't shatter from the heat. The ceremony was brief and the celebration was merry. The food was delicious and the music was pretty good for a tape deck running on a car battery.

Carole and Mike only spent a little over a four hundred dollars for their handfasting, but they had put in hundreds of hours of work. They had the ceremony and celebration that they wanted by investing hours of careful planning, checking, and rechecking with people who had made commitments to help and by making backup plans in case something or someone didn't come through. They had spent heavily of their time budget but had been able to economize on their money budget. The emotional outlay had been minimal. Carole and

Mike found that the effort and work was worth it: They got the country meadow ceremony that *both* of them had dreamed of having.

A Disaster Made in Illusions

Now, let's look at another real-life incident. Chris and Vince thought they wanted a simple homemade wedding. But they both had jobs that required some weekend and night work and they both had children from previous marriages. Vince was known to be in deadly danger if he so much as picked up a screwdriver or a saucepan. As for Chris, she had once taken a course in sewing but the only thing she was able to stitch was her finger. They both admitted that, in all honesty, they couldn't do much of the work in preparing for the handfasting, and so they turned to friends and relatives for help.

Unfortunately, Chris was *extremely* unclear about what she wanted, and thus sent very confusing signals to the people who had agreed to help her. And whenever she would ask Vince for advice or suggestions he just shrugged and said "It's up to you, honey." Much later I learned that he believed that what he wanted wasn't appropriate for a Pagan ceremony.

Although they had budgeted more than nine months to prepare for the event, nothing got done on schedule. A lot of money was squandered as Chris changed her mind and then changed it again. This alienated both friends and family who saw their time and their resources being wasted. More than one person walked away in disgust.

Chris's confusing signals resulted not only in miscommunication and in money misspent; it also had a serious impact on the emotion quotient. Headaches, upset stomachs, quivering exhaustion, temper tantrums, and shouting matches took their toll on Chris, Vince, and everyone around them. Not only was this very bad energy to be bringing into a handfasting ceremony, but the entire occasion created serious relationship rifts within Chris's family.

Chris *thought* she wanted a simple ceremony outdoors in her mother's garden. She never considered that her mother, a Pagan-friendly but still nominally Christian person, might be uncomfortable with that idea. The woman's yard was small and she was surrounded by neighbors who would be justifiably interested in the "odd goings-on over at the Windsors'." Chris assumed that her aunt—a woman who adored gardening—would allow Chris to take all the flowers she wanted for the ceremony and the celebration. But Chris never asked—she simply assumed.

Chris asked a cousin to make her a simple handfasting dress of cotton—"Something she could wear again"—but when they went to the fabric store, the only fabrics that Chris truly wanted to look at were the silks and satins. The relative bought the cotton that Chris eventually chose, but Chris had nothing but criticism for the dress the woman finally sewed. I remember a fight in which the cousin flung the dress in Chris's face and stomped out. Chris still couldn't understand what was wrong.

When Vince asked her what she wanted him and his groomsmen to wear, she told him to wear something "nice." Chris was heartbroken when he decided on a pair of dark pants and a colorful shirt. By the time we got her to admit she wanted tuxedos, it was too late to rent anything that she liked. In fact, it was too late to do *anything* that Chris liked.

In the end the discord proved too great: Two weeks before the ceremony, Chris's mother had a heart attack—probably brought on in part by the tension and stress of the daily battles she was having with Chris. The poor woman was in intensive care for four days.

At this point I told Chris that I would not facilitate any handfasting ceremony in which the energies were so twisted and angry. It was a certain failure. When I tried to explain to her that what she *thought* she wanted and what she really desired were far apart, she became almost hysterical. I ended up shrugging my shoulders and letting her be.

Chris and Vince were married by a justice of the peace, and to this day Chris has not forgiven her mother, her aunt, her cousin, or me—a very sad ending to what had started out to be a joyous occasion.

Why had Mike and Carole's handfasting been a dream come true while Vince and Chris's turned into their worst nightmare?

Because Mike and Carole were honest about what they wanted and they communicated their desires clearly to the people around them.

Chris was not honest about her desires and she miscommunicated so badly that more than her handfasting was ruined. And that self-honesty or lack thereof was the root of Chris's problem: The most important person whom Chris deluded was *herself.*

Looking back, it became very apparent that the problems that Chris and Vince experienced were buried deep in a pile of "shoulds and ought-tos." As a child, Chris had dreamed of a wedding with a big white dress, lovely arranged bouquets of white roses and lilacs, and a sit-down reception. Yet when Chris began to make plans for her handfasting with Vince, she suppressed her lifelong dreams and desires with ideas she felt were more "acceptably Pagan." She thought that she *should* want a simple outdoor ceremony. She had the idea that that was the Pagan way to do it. When she tried to impose the shoulds upon her wants, she got a disaster.

Now, as we shall see later, Chris could have had all of what she really desired and had it in a Pagan way if only she had been honest with her dreams.

Remember Chris when you begin to plan your handfasting: ask yourself what you see when you imagine *your* perfect celebration and ceremony. Not anybody else's; not what is considered Pagan Politically Correct; not what your Pagan friends think you *should* have. This is all about what YOU want.

Hired Events

If things for your handfasting have to be exactly the way you want them (and why not?), then decide exactly what you want from each service provider (florists, caterer, photographer) and how you want it and write it out carefully, stipulating every detail. Then submit your lists to an assortment of vendors and ask them each to bid on your event. Give them a certain period of tme to come up with a price and then collect the bids. Once you've picked your providers, have contracts drawn up—and approach the contracts as if you were a lawyer—read the fine print! And when hiring services and purchasing products, remember: if it seems too good to be true, it probably is. Cheapest isn't always the way to go, but neither is expensive.

When considering hiring services from non-Pagans who might become frightened or have religious conflicts with a Pagan ceremony, a good way to ascertain if they'll be okay is to invite them to a low-key ritual. Make it clear that attendance is mandatory if you are to consider their bid. When they attend, carefully assess their reactions to the energies of the ritual. If they are comfortable and still interested in bidding, they are a good prospect. Keep in mind: If the best photographer or florist in town does not wish to "waste time" being interviewed or assessed, you don't want them at your hand-fasting. You shouldn't have to be preoccupied with their needs and desires in order to get top quality services. This is where a generous time budget is very useful: It gives you room to shop wisely.

Saving Money on Goods and Services

Some of the best ways to save money follow.

INVITATIONS   Consider making your own invitations. There is plenty of beautiful stationery out there that is compatible with computer printers, and you will need to customize the invitation anyway. If you can keep invitations simple or you don't need people to send back RSVP cards, send pretty postcards. And remember—your invitations *do not* need to be hand addressed. You have better things to do with your time and no one who has any sense will care. Use a label or envelope-printing program and a database of all the invitees.

FOOD   Don't blow your budget on an expensive meal. Banquet-hall food is mediocre at best. Unless you're willing to spend a considerable amount of time overseeing the chef and whoever is doing the food purchasing, any food you get will be so-so in taste and quality. This is one area where having a couple of good cooks in your circle of family and friends can make a really big difference—just make certain that they buy the best and freshest ingredients you can afford. In addition, keeping the menu simple makes for happy helpers and satisfied guests. Foods that slop (like soup) should be avoided, as well as anything that might drip (such as barbecued ribs) unless you can't imagine a celebration without them—then provide a lot of napkins!

ALCOHOLIC BEVERAGES   Having an open bar is extremely expensive, and you end up paying all that money for low-quality liquor. And in truth, no one needs to get drunk at your handfasting; it isn't in keeping with the meaning of the ceremony. Wine and soft drinks are all that are necessary. And you may wish to leave out the wine.

DRESSES AND COSTUMES   Your dresses and costumes are not usually the best place to scrimp, and you should let someone hand-make your dress *only* if you know a very competent seamstress. The best inexpensive alternative is to *rent* a dress. You can rent a perfectly immaculate and fashionable dress in almost any size. By renting you are also spared the rather large expense of getting your gown cleaned and preserved after the ceremony—and you won't have to lug a huge cardboard box about with you as you move from house to house.

While there is something very romantic about owning your dress don't beguile yourself into believing that anyone—including your daughters—will want to wear it "someday when."

Another very good alternative is to think of your handfasting clothes as the costumes they actually are. Costumes do not have a lot of expensive handiwork; they use facade and illusion and your handfasting dress can be made more affordable by using those techniques.

RINGS   Don't be deceived by the diamond industry's claims of diamonds as being a good investment. Unless the stone is very large—in excess of one carat—and is of the first water, that diamond is not going to appreciate in value. On the other hand, beautiful Celtic knotwork rings can be found in many different catalogs and can be sized to a perfect fit by any jeweler. An afternoon poking around a flea market or looking through antiques stores can result in finding unique and perfect treasures. And, if you fancy the really homemade approach, you can make your own rings out of twisted wire. Fire Mountain, in Denver, Colorado, is a reputable jewelry-supply company that sells both sterling silver and gold wire, as well as the jigs for wrapping and books on how to do it. Just be careful, making jewelry can become addictive.

When Not to Scrimp

There are certain goods and services that are going to cost a lot but are worth it.

Photographers   A good photographer is going to be expensive, but it's usually worth every cent. There will only be one opportunity to immortalize your moment, so don't take chances with cheap photographers or with "Uncle Dan who is pretty good with a camera." Avoid photographers who want to sell you a package. These people usually don't know how to compose a picture, frame it with light or shadow, or integrate the elements of the scene into a harmonious whole. All they know is how to follow a formula: "Take two shots of bride with her parents, two of groom with his parents, two of the garter, three of the first dance . . ."

A good photographer is an artist who will approach his or her task with more than just a desire to get the job done. Be prepared to pay.

You may be able to economize on the photography if you live near a fine arts college. Often students of photography will be willing to take the pictures for a reasonable charge and give you the negatives for you to develop as you wish. What is a reasonable charge? Here on the mid-Atlantic coast even a first-year student would feel insulted if you paid them less than a hundred dollars plus the cost of film. But make certain that even with students you have a well-written contract and some way of redress should they lose the film or decide to withhold it. And *always* ask to see a portfolio of previous work, whether you go with a student or a seasoned pro.

MUSICIANS   If you are going to have live music don't ask your friends to provide it. They want to enjoy the party too. Hiring a band or a string group needs to be done far in advance of the date of the handfasting. You will be required to give them a *nonrefundable* deposit—and even if one of the couple dies, that deposit will not come back.

Musicians are artists, and good ones give you more than just tunes that are easy to listen to and enjoyable to dance to— they put a little bit of magickal energy into every note they play. That magick is going to have a hefty price tag.

The best way to get around this sizable outlay of cash is to hire a DJ (and be sure to go through the same hiring process as with the other service providers). You can also buy a nice portable CD player that will hold more than one CD at a time. You will spend less on the CD player and a dozen new CDs than you will for the DJ. And you'll have the CD player the next day. Since many people already own a CD player, purchasing some new CDs is usually all that is necessary.

It is often best to use recorded music for the ceremony— although this is the one area where it is suitable to ask musical friends to contribute. Just ensure they have ample time to practice the selections that you and your coven leaders agree on. (See chapter 13 for musical selections and sources.)

HAIRCUTS   Get the best haircut you can afford three or four weeks in advance of the handfasting date and then hide the scissors.

Threaten anyone who wants to get "creative" with their hair with a poppet full of needles. (This is also true for tattoos!) For some unknown reason (probably an innate desire to mark the spiritual passage with something physical), people often attempt to trim or modify their hair or body right before a big ceremony or ritual. Being aware of that propensity can spare you a lot of heartache. (I knew a young bride who had her nose pierced three days before her wedding. Unfortunately, it became seriously infected, and she had a schnoz redder than Rudolph the Reindeer's on her big day.)

If the women in the party are going to have their hair styled by professional hairdressers, schedule two sessions: one several weeks in advance of the handfasting date and one the day before or the morning of the rite. On the first session let the professional brainstorm and then, when you and the hairdresser agree on what you like, tip the person lavishly and make sure that that *very same person* will be the one who will style your hair before the handfasting. This is not a service that should be lowballed, and even though your best friend André is a probably wonderful hairdresser, if he is in the handfasting party, he will be too nervous to do a good job. Hire someone who is not emotionally involved.

6

CHOOSING A SITE FOR YOUR HANDFASTING AND CELEBRATION

Choosing where you will hold your handfasting and celebration is one of the most important parts of the planning process. If you want to save yourself time, money, and tears, it is essential to first know exactly what type of celebration (in terms of food, number of guests, choice of band or DJ, and so on) you want *before* you even start looking.

It is easy to become seduced by the charms of a site that, while lovely and probably perfect for someone else, is just not right for you. You won't be the first person to fall under the spell of the event planner's enthusiasm and find yourself writing out a check for an unsuitable site, one that forces you to go back and undo months of planning. So don't do it. Don't play that game. Instead of seeing a site and planning your ceremony and celebration to fit it, plan the ceremony and celebration and then go find the best site for your needs.

Here are some examples of how this approach can save you a bucket of misery.

Misery or Happiness: What You Buy Is What You Get

Mary and Pete

Mary and Pete had just started their own business, which was doing well. However, they didn't have a lot of money to play with, so they decided on a small handfasting and celebration. The guest list was up to about forty people, and the couple was considering the local fire department's hall. They were certain that they wanted to keep things simple. Then Mary's mother insisted they "just take a look at" the Coventry Hills Banquet Hall that had just been built a few miles from her house.

The place was beautiful. It had sparkling fountains and mirrored rooms and cozy little gazebos and a lovely formal garden. The banquet room could easily hold two hundred people. The servers were trained performers (they sang, danced, juggled . . .) and the menu was . . . well, enticing.

Before Mary and Pete knew what was happening, they were planning their handfasting and celebration to take advantage of the Coventry Banquet Hall facilities—and since there was room for two hundred people, there was no reason to limit the guest list.

After they had signed the contract and paid the deposit, they discovered to their great chagrin and dismay that the only item of food that could be cooked off premises and then brought in was the cake—and even that was frowned upon by the staff. The food they had been shown and allowed to taste had come from the "premiere" menu. The menu they could afford was pathetic.

Because of the exquisiteness of the setting, Mary changed her plans for her dress, and Pete and his friends rented tuxedos. Every time they turned around, the catering manager or facilities manager of the Coventry Hills Banquet Hall was urging them to commit to spending more and more money on ridiculous items, like matches and toilet paper printed with their names and the date of their ceremony!

Since the hall maintained control over the flowers, the music, and the parking (there was a fee!) Pete and Mary found that there were few ways to economize. Thus the couple, with the help of Mary's mother (I will give her credit, she put her money on the line) spent a fortune they could ill afford—and then they found out that the ritual had to be held elsewhere. At the last moment, the manager of the hall decided he was uncomfortable with a Pagan ceremony being performed on his property, and felt that it might have a bad effect on the image for the hall he was trying to build. Had they wanted to, they could have taken the Coventry Hills Banquet Hall to court for what I considered a breach of contract, but by then they were too tired and too broke to contest the matter. To quote them: "We just want to get it over with!"

The day of the ceremony was rainy, so Pete and Mary ended up having their ceremony in Mary's parents' basement. By the time they arrived at the hall for the reception everyone was in a disgruntled mood. The music provided by the hall was not the music they had stipulated in their agreement—the manager felt he could get away with switching services on the "bikers"—and the food was awful. (I personally went to a fast-food restaurant afterward.) Mary, Pete, and their guests were hurried out of the rooms they had rented long before their time was up.

Learn from Pete and Mary's disaster: Don't let the context decide the content.

Liz and Joe

Liz and Joe decided on a winter event with a medieval theme for their handfasting and celebration with costumes and an authentic menu. They decided on all the particulars first and then went searching for a suitable site. Since the Yule season is a busy and expensive time, they chose January as the month for their handfasting.

They found a large firemen's hall that had no restrictions on decorations (other than anything that was a clear fire hazard), a clean serviceable kitchen, a staff they could hire if they wished, and a pretty deck in the back that could serve as a ceremony site.

One of Liz's friends was a prop manager for the local community theater. With a little thought, he came up with a simple and affordable design to make the walls of the hall look like stone. Banners made of felt to which Celtic Pagan symbols were glued covered the biggest eyesores, and two long cardboard "windows" painted to appear to be looking out over a snowy meadow were placed on either side of a dais made from plywood and two-by-fours. White sheets bought at a discount store and trimmed with glued-on symbols made of felt covered the tables.

With white Christmas tree lights strung along the edges of the ceiling, fresh cut ivy and holly, a few florist flowers and candles inside jars on the tables, and a fake fireplace with a "flaming" log (rented from a prop shop) in one corner, the place became a wonderland.

Joe found an SCA (Society for Creative Anachronism) group that was willing to provide medieval music and that would perform in authentic costumes. All of the guests were urged to rent costumes—which they did cheerfully—and Joe and his groomsmen rented "armor" instead of tuxedos. Liz's and her maids' dresses were the only costly things about the entire event. Liz's dress was white silk velvet and cost about four hundred dollars, which included the seamstress's fee. Her maids wore green velveteen dresses, which cost under a hundred dollars apiece.

The ceremony was held outside on the deck, recalling the old custom of marrying on the steps, and because it was snowing, the Rite of Handfasting was kept to little more than the solemn essentials. Candles in tall glasses shone in the purple evening air and each bridesmaid held a candle in her ivy and white rose bouquet. Every member of the party wore cloaks and their Pagan jewelry glittered on dark wool and velvet.

As the guests and the members of the bridal party went inside the hall, they were greeted with cups of warm cider and the smell of cooking food.

The service was competent and friendly—and one of the waiters got into the spirit of things and wore a costume. The food—most of it cooked by Liz and her mother—was not terribly authentic but it was delicious. We danced reels and line dances until it was time to leave, and even then the custodian said, "What the heck!" and joined in for another hour of merriment and dancing. It was a memorable ceremony and celebration. Even now, after seven years, we look at the pictures and remember what a wonderful time we had.

Liz and Joe would have been able to find any number of places in which their plans could work: VFW halls, Masonic temples (check these carefully—some have religious restrictions) and Unitarian churches, to name a few. But the important thing is that they decided on the *content* of the wedding before they looked at sites and thus were able resist the enticing seduction of the commercial halls and banquet rooms.

A good thought to keep in mind is this: Is renting this site the sole way in which this establishment makes its money? Or is it a way for the establishment to *supplement* its income?

If it is the sole manner in which the money is made, be aware that everything, from the food down to the matches with which you light the candles, will have a cost. The establishment will want to have complete control over what is spent. And the facility manager will be eager to have you spend a lot.

If, on the other hand, the establishment exists to serve another purpose (like a VFW) and rents out the hall to supplement its income, it is far more likely to be flexible. Not every banqueting hall experience is as ghastly as Pete and Mary's; not every fireman's hall is as wonderful as Joe and Liz's. But, in general, the more control you have, the better you will enjoy your ceremony and celebration.

Finding Happiness in Your Own Backyard

Of course, the place that will cost the least and where you will have the most control is in your own backyard. It will also have some severe restrictions. Many Pagans have a vision of a perfect ceremony in a lovely flowered meadow, with a clear blue sky and only a few butterflies flitting about. Unfortunately, those perfect conditions are seldom experienced in reality. Think about the last picnic you attended.

The first consideration is feeling safe. Consider carefully before planning a Pagan ritual in your backyard or that of a relative or friend. Will the neighbors be understanding or will they make trouble? Your handfasting is only one day out of many—consider carefully what you are willing to risk. Having to find a new house and a new neighborhood is a frightful expense.

The second consideration will be the limits the space will put on your guest list. Unless you live on a large estate, it's a little difficult to have a sit-down dinner for a hundred people. (Actually, I did it once and it worked on my little acre, but it was tight.) Even with having the food made in advance, or catered, a normal (nonprofessional) kitchen has limits on its capabilities, as well as the number of people who can work in it effectively. I actually fed almost a hundred people at my son's handfasting but I had the help of many competent people. However, it is not something I would recommend to someone who doesn't know a spatula from a blender.

Be sure to consider parking facilities—if a guest should block a neighbor's driveway, you may be risking an ugly feud. Some neighborhoods have restrictions on how many nonresident vehicles can be parked on the streets at any given time. I once knew a groom whose car was towed while he was cutting his wedding cake. And keep in mind that access to the site will need to be kept clear in case of fire or an accident.

Don't ignore the fire hazards inherent in a large group of people. Make allowances for those people who still insist on smoking.

And *never* underestimate the weight of a crowd of fifty on a deck built for ten. Not too long ago, in a town near where I live, a wedding turned into a terrible tragedy when the deck holding the entire wedding party and many guests collapsed. Four people were killed, including the groom. It isn't just outside decks that have limitations—I have heard of living-room floors falling into basements under the weight of too many people.

Remember to take into account the limitations of the sewer or septic system in your house. Sinks clogging and toilets overflowing are common occurrences at big parties. Be prepared to call the plumber or the septic system service.

Also—and while awkward, this is necessary—if you are having the celebration in a home filled with family treasures, be prepared to pack up and store most of the valuables. It will protect them from being damaged—or worse—from disappearing. Theft is not a crime restricted to the non-Pagans.

Tents should be erected by the professionals from the service from which you are renting them: Those companies carry insurance that will cover your losses if one of the tents collapses and someone is hurt. Remember that in the summer the air inside such tents can become stifling. Plan on ways to move the air about—in hot climates you should consider air-conditioning.

The same cautions pertain to outdoor sanitary facilities. Portapotties should be rented and serviced by professionals. Be sure to rent one portapotty for every thirty or forty people you invite. Nothing is more disgusting than a portapotty used beyond its capacity. Don't place them in the full sun and don't make them impossible to find.

Bugs and stinging insects are naturally attracted to food being served outside. Food fouled by insects is not appealing. Spraying with a nontoxic spray (try Knockdown) the morning of the event is a good idea. Setting bait jars to lure any bugs away from the food can also work. You will also need to make certain that there are sufficient ways of maintaining the temperature of any food served because food poisoning would be a real disaster at a handfasting and celebration.

Try to arrange for the lawn to be mowed several days in advance of your celebration: the effects of allergens will be less, and any gopher holes that might sprain ankles and break legs will be more easily spotted and corrected. When the celebration is going to last into the night, develop a lighting strategy that will prevent people from falling over items hidden in the shadows or into holes or ditches. Broken limbs can result in nasty lawsuits.

Some people take out umbrella insurance policies before hosting large parties at their homes or the homes of friends. I highly recommend that you investigate such a policy if your celebration site has any hazards such as stairs and paved walkways, waterways or ponds, trees or shrubs that could drop branches—the list is almost endless. An important point, and one far too often overlooked, is that accidents happen and with today's medical costs insuring that lawsuits are certain to follow, you cannot afford to be without insurance.

And always—PLAN FOR RAIN.

By now you will have surmised that I have a bias against outdoor ceremonies. You are correct. My experience has been that there are too many things that can go wrong and too many factors that cannot be controlled (such as the weather). At least, that is what the practical person in me says.

However, the Witch in me exclaims, "Where else *could* we do it? Outdoors, under the natural roof of heaven, with a carpet of grass, and trees as walls is the most natural and beautiful and sacred place!" So even with the liabilities I have mentioned, it is certain that most Pagans will want to have their ceremony and celebration outside. And almost all of the handfastings I have facilitated have been outdoors—including my son's, a rather large and elegant affair that turned my backyard into a fairyland for a single enchanted day.

An outdoor ceremony is definitely Pagan. It is almost the defining factor for many people. So . . . if you decide on an outdoor ceremony, your date will be constrained by the season of the year. And you must be realistic about the weather. I can recall one couple that insisted on having an outside ceremony in a public park during the late fall. The bride nearly froze to death. I wore electric socks and boots under my vestments. If you are determined on having an outdoor winter wedding make the ceremony short and sweet and the reception hall warm and nearby.

Except for the lucky inhabitants of tropical areas, late spring to early fall are the best target times for outdoor ceremonies. Whichever month and day you choose, the most important thing you will have to do for an outdoor ceremony and celebration will be to plan for rain.

PLAN FOR RAIN.

I do not think that concept can be overemphasized enough. More than one handfasting has become a soggy mess because the couple did not plan for rain.

Don't rely on weather magick—you will have far too many things on your mind—and too many calls on your energies to ensure that the weather magick is effective. And few other people have the resources to bring a sufficient amount of energy to bear. I have done weather magick—it does succeed but needs to be started months before the date of the handfasting, and worked on with complete concentration several times a day, every day. Consider carefully before you attempt that sort of commitment.

As with any manipulative magicks, there are ethical considerations that must be considered before doing weather magick.

These ethics apply in the case of handfastings just as they would in every other instance in which it would be convenient to control the weather. Doing weather magick so that you can have sunny skies for your ceremony might be a very selfish and mean-spirited thing to do to the rest of the biosystems in your area. And the three-fold return could be ugly indeed. So amend the above statement so that it reads: PLAN FOR RAIN AND DON'T MESS WITH THE WEATHER!

Another item of concern is insects. I recently was told of a ceremony that came to an abrupt halt when the bride was stung by a hornet attracted to the flowers in her bouquet. Dangerously allergic, she was rushed to the hospital and took days to recover. Bees, hornets, gnats, and mosquitos don't know that you are having an important ceremony. That flowery meadow or beautiful park or grassy backyard is their home—their feeding range—and they aren't going to vacate it for your convenience.

Citronella and DEET may not be the most attractive smells but they can make an outdoor ceremony much safer and much more comfortable. I recommend that you avoid highly scented flowers if the people concerned have allergies to insect stings and use colors sparingly that attract insects (insects love yellow). Make certain that an insect allergy kit is available and that someone knows how to use it, especially if a person who is allergic to insect bites is present at the ceremony.

7

PLANNING
THE HANDFASTING
OF YOUR DREAMS

I keep stressing that the ceremony and celebration are about you: the couple getting handfasted. I will continue to stress that concept for the following reason: as soon as someone whispers "wedding" or "handfasting," everyone comes running with *their* ideas, *their* dreams and *their* wishes and wants. The emotional context of a handfasting is such that many people don't understand the inappropriateness of imposing their desires and wishes into another person's life. Acceding to those exterior desires often makes for long-lasting discomfort, resentment, and unhappiness. Perhaps one of the best reasons the couple should pay for their own handfasting is that this way no one else can control the choices by controlling the purse strings.

However, you haven't lived in a vacuum—you and your beloved have been exposed to many different concepts about marriages and weddings. You probably don't have a clear focus on just one idea. Most likely, you have several—and they are all appealing in their separate and special ways. So how do you make your choices?

Following is a worksheet that you will find helpful. Make four or five copies so that you can write out several different versions of what you might like. Don't try to do it with only one sheet. There is something magic about writing an idea or plan down on paper; as you do so it becomes more real—almost palpable—and difficult to change. So give yourself a lot of different canvases on which to paint your perfect fantasy.

Allow yourself to brainstorm—write down every crazy idea—from getting handfasted in a hot-air balloon to a scuba ceremony in the Caribbean. Then, spread each form out on the kitchen table and consider them.

You won't find much on this list that is different from the lists found in guides for traditional weddings. It's practical, and I have found that practicality now usually equates to enjoyability later.

And don't forget to budget in time for the meditations and trance workings to help you decide what you want and how you are going to do it. After all, a handfasting is a very magickal event . . . so use your magick to help plan it.

HANDFASTING WISH LIST

Kind of Ceremony We Want _____

Date of Ceremony and Reception _____

Date of Rehearsal _____

Location of Ceremony _____

Location of Rehearsal _____

Options in Case of Rain _____

Type of Celebration/Reception We Want _____

_____

Location of Celebration/Reception _____

Options in Case of Rain _____

Name of Facilitating Priest _____

Address and Phone Number _____

_____

E-Mail Address _____

Name of Facilitating Priestess _____

Address and Phone Number _____

_____

E-Mail Address _____

Theme of Ceremony and Celebration (if any)

_____

Type of Dress for Women _____

Head Covering/Veil _____

Type of Dress for Men _____

Bride's Attendants _____

Addresses _____

_____

_____

_____

Phone Numbers

_____

E-Mail Addresses _____

Groom's Attendants _____

Addresses _____

_____

_____

Phone Numbers

_____

E-Mail Addresses _____

Lodging Facilities for Out-of-Town Attendants and Guests

_____

_____

_____

Food for Ceremony _____

Provider _____

Food for Celebration _____

_____

_____

_____

_____

Provider(s)_____

_____

Wine (or substitute) for Ceremony _____

Flowers for Altar _____

Provider_____

Flowers for Bride and Attendants

_____

_____

_____

_____

Provider_____

Flowers for Groom and Attendants

_____

_____

_____

_____

Provider_____

Candles for Ceremony _____

Provider_____

Ritual Objects for Ceremony _____

_____

Provider_____

Flowers for Celebration

_____

_____

_____

_____

Flowers for Parents and Other Special People

_____

_____

_____

_____

Provider _____

Music for Ceremony _____

_____

_____

_____

Backup_____

Music for Celebration _____

_____

_____

_____

Backup _____

Photographer for Ceremony _____

Backup _____

Photographer for Celebration _____

Backup _____

Transportation to Ceremony

_____

_____

Backup _____

Transportation to Celebration _____

_____

Backup _____

Dates Available for Meditations _____

Dates Available for Enhancing Rituals _____

_____

Wording on Invitations_____

_____

_____

_____

_____

The *Big* Handfasting—the Pagan Way

Kathy and Jim wanted a very big ceremony and an even bigger celebration. They spent a little over a year planning for their handfasting. The dress alone took nine months to sew, bead, and embroider. I should know. I made it.

Kathy and Jim encountered their share of problems but those problems came not from miscommunication or delusion. Their problems arouse out of prejudice and religious intolerance.

Jim was a nominal Catholic, Kathy was an initiated Witch. They had a lot of compromising to do. In particular, Jim was thrown up against his religion's absolute intolerance of Kathy's belief system. Kathy found she had an almost inchoate anger at authoritarian belief systems. Yet when I warned them that they were up against some serious religious intolerance both Jim and Kathy found that concept difficult to accept—after all, these were modern times and religious persecutions were things of the past. Weren't they?

Both Kathy and Jim were shocked and hurt when they discovered that religious intolerance, bigotry, and hypocrisy were alive and well in the late twentieth century. While Kathy's coven leaders weren't too happy about including Christian elements in the ceremony, the Catholic priest refused to cooperate in any way whatsoever. In truth the man had nothing to say about it, since he was merely following the rigid dogmatic intolerance that has been a part of the Catholic Church for two thousand years. And while that intolerance astounded Jim and outraged Kathy, it was exactly what I had expected.

After weeks of agonized searching and deliberations, I suggested they have two ceremonies: one Catholic and one Pagan. Again, the Catholic priest refused to cooperate: there could be *no* Pagan ceremony. Then it was Jim's turn to compromise. He decided that the priest didn't have to know about the Pagan ceremony.

Kathy sat through the Catholic prenuptial classes with her mouth clamped tightly shut. After each class she would vent her ridicule and her scathing comments on the belief system, dumping them onto poor Jim's shoulders. On the other hand, Jim was humbled by his church's attitude and overwhelmed by Kathy's brutal response. Given the situation, Jim's tactics were deceptive and not exactly honorable, but the intolerance of the Catholic Church seemed to make the deception inevitable.

When I asked Jim why he was so desperate to have a Catholic ceremony that he was willing to deceive the priest, he started thinking. Jim began seriously questioning his religious affiliations. Still, he believed that the Catholic ceremony was necessary for the comfort of his parents and relatives. They had given Jim the impression that for them a Pagan ceremony would not constitute a valid marriage. (As it later turned out, that impression was an illusion but at the time there was no way that Jim could have known it.)

The Catholic ceremony was held in the morning; the Pagan ceremony was held at sunset on the same day. Kathy and Jim rented an entire summer camp—with all of the recreational facilities included—for the location of both the Pagan ceremony and the reception. They provided a lunch after the guests arrived after driving almost thirty miles from the Catholic church to the summer camp, and then, in the evening after the Pagan Handfasting, there was a sit-down dinner of steak and lobster followed by dancing in an open-air pavilion bespangled with tiny crystal lights.

Kathy and Jim admitted they spent a modest fortune but they got the marriage and handfasting ceremonies that they wanted. In fact, the only flaw was that the photographer became seriously frightened by the energies of the Pagan ceremony and he took all of the pictures from many, many feet away. Yet, all in all, the whole celebratory event was splendid.

Like Mike and Carole, Kathy and Jim had the kind of handfasting ceremony and celebration that they wanted because they were honest and clear about their desires, they communicated openly (except to the Catholic priest), and they worked hard to bring their handfasting and celebration into existence.

Kathy and Jim spent lavishly from all their budgets—time, money, and emotion. Many hours of sewing, beading, cooking, baking, arranging flowers, picking out music, fighting and reconciling, crying and laughing went into the making of a memorable occasion. Thousands of dollars were spent providing for the many services that time wouldn't buy. And both Kathy and Jim underwent some serious emotional growth that—painful as it was at the time—has stood them in good stead in the years since their handfasting.

So if your dream has always been a beautiful white dress with a long train and a half dozen maids in gorgeous gowns, *do it*. If you want it outside, *do it*. If you get grass stains on the gown (unless you have rented it) what does it matter? You will never wear the gown again and it is highly unlikely that anyone else will either, so go ahead and enjoy it.

If you have always dreamed of having your father walk you down the aisle, *do it*. Just make certain that your mother does too. If you want organ music, rent an electric organ, set it on a rubber mat (so the organist doesn't get shocked if the ground is damp), and *do it!*

Roses and crystal and champagne fountains, if they are your dream, they are magickal—so *do it*.

8

DEALING WITH
PAINFUL DIFFERENCES

In the last chapter I described the pain and stress that Kathy
and Jim experienced when they were confronted with the
dogma of the Roman Catholic church. Most Pagans have a
flexible and open attitude about the differences among belief
systems, and they are often astonished and sometimes angered
when they discover that other religions don't have the same
mindset. It is important to understand that the resolution of
this issue is not up to the minister, priest, or rabbi. The rules
and canon law are firmly embedded in the dogma of the particular religion and there is little or nothing that any one
clergy member can do to change it. As a priest once said to
me, "I don't want to be intolerant—my faith requires it of me."

Remember when you first discovered you were a Pagan and told your friends and acquaintances? Remember how some of them thought you were being silly, or joking? That is a common response from family and friends when a couple announces they are going to be handfasted.

Some people get scared, others think you're jesting, and still others don't take it seriously and think you'll come to your senses and "do it right."

Even when the Christian and Jewish clergy are motivated by their own liberal ethics to work with you, they often try to force a monotheistic mold onto Pagan beliefs. You can accede to this, or you may calmly and firmly insist on the multiplicity of your beliefs. It is up to you to decide how much their participation matters to you. In my experience, the participation of traditional clergy has rarely enhanced any handfasting, simply because the people with whom I was dealing did not respect my gods in the same way they expected me to respect theirs. It is a sad fact that much of our culture and legal system is based on upholding their beliefs while regulating Pagan beliefs to either fantasy or evil.

At almost every Pagan handfasting that I have facilitated or attended has had problems involving the collision of belief systems. People have been noisy and disrespectful during the ritual, some relatives have refused to attend, and one father actually attempted to have his daughter *deprogrammed* when he found out she was going to be handfasted. I have had couples make the serious mistake of not telling people that the ceremony they would be attending is a Pagan handfasting, mistakenly thinking that once the guests were seated in the room they would behave. They don't—they make angry commotions and get up and leave. One young woman did not tell her mother the true nature of the ceremony until everyone arrived at the gothic castle for the rehearsal. The woman was outraged, and rightly so, for she had spent thousands of dollars trying to give her daughter what she thought the young woman wanted, only to find out that her daughter did not trust her enough to tell her that she was Pagan.

Only after long hours of talk with the mother did I agree to continue. I felt as betrayed as the bride's mother did. I had asked Susy several times to bring her mother to the planning sessions and she always had a last-minute excuse why her mother wasn't going to be there. Such deceitfulness is not a good way to start a union, and is very bad energy to bring into the magickal rite of handfasting.

Some couples hand out information sheets explaining the ritual and the Pagan meanings. (See Appendix II for an example I have included.) Doing this is a good idea, especially if most of the guests are open-minded or Pagan friendly. It is *essential* when your list includes friends and relatives who don't have the slightest inkling of what is going on. Be aware, though, that this information won't defuse some instances of ignorance and prejudice. Jim and Kathy actually had a guest—the father of the maid of honor—who in the middle of the ritual loudly declared that it was blasphemous and evil!

Some couples try to remove the more distinctive Pagan elements from their ritual, and then wonder why the ceremony turned out "so flat . . . almost boring." However, this can work; just be clear that it is what *you* want, and it's not being imposed on you by a belief that you should not rock the boat on your handfasting day.

You, too, will most likely have to deal with religious intolerance. The marital codes of most states make that certain. And that intolerance will be an annoyance and a hindrance or worse. Sometimes an extremely painful confrontation with intolerance can almost destroy the happiness of the event.

So, what can you do?

First, the most important thing you can do is to be absolutely honest and up front about the nature of your religion and your handfasting. If you don't want to do that, *don't* have a handfasting. Give your relatives and friends the kind of ceremony they want and deal with your own sense of being let-down later.

People who have been invited to a "new-agey kind of thing" may well become angry and resentful if they find they have been duped—lured to attend an event that, had they known its true nature, they would have declined. Don't issue standard invitations and then not deliver on the standard ceremony. It is bad manners and worse magick.

Second, don't water your ritual down to where you can't "taste" it. Serve it full strength or don't serve it. People can sense when something deceitful is being presented to them. Again, they may walk away with a bad taste in their mouth and a bad opinion of you.

Third, make a list of people who you think are likely to cause problems. Then make some hard decisions: is it really necessary to invite these people? Is it possible to talk to them in advance, explaining what you are going to do and why, and then assess whether or not they should be asked to attend? Perhaps they would be willing to attend a Pagan event—such as an open ritual or a performance by a Pagan group weeks before the Handfasting. If they are comfortable with that kind of thing, they will most likely be comfortable at your ritual and celebration. They may be sensitive enough to appreciate that you are allowing them to experience growth in a gentle manner.

It's really difficult when the problem guests are the ones who matter the most. Parents and grandparents who are in conflict with your belief systems can be very difficult. However, since handfastings are about growth, shedding the old and taking on the new, perhaps this is the best time to gently but firmly explain to them that it is your ritual, you are paying for it, and you are planning it. Make a clear position: they can participate willingly, they can be polite guests, or they can stay away. Then for your sanity and theirs, close the discussion and stand by your decision.

Mothers find this attitude hard to accept. Most women have had to endure having *their* mothers run *their* weddings, so they don't understand why they won't be allowed to dictate the ritual and celebration for their own children. They become angry and rejected when they are not allowed to "run the show."

Fathers can be very difficult also. They may view the Pagan belief system of their child as a flouting of responsibility to the family name and honor, or as a rebellion against parental authority. Many parents use the nuptials of their children to pay off social debts, display wealth, and increase their social standing. In honesty, weddings for this purpose are not for the couple involved. In fact, the whole thing would serve the parents' purposes equally well if two stuffed dummies were propped up in front of the assembled guests. If you have this type of parent, you are in a difficult place and I can only hope that the courage that comes from your convictions and beliefs can carry you through.

The most common difficulty is that the man and woman who are going to be handfasted don't want to hurt their parents; they really want their parents to be involved in their happiness and they want what they suppose "other people have" . . . a happy participation in the event by the parents.

But if the parents' beliefs are in conflict with Pagan beliefs, that isn't going to happen. And accepting that fact is essential in handling the resulting emotional tidal waves with confidence and serenity. When people see that you really mean what you say and that you are not going to shoulder the misplacement of their responsibility for their feelings and actions, they usually become more willing to cooperate.

What I am going to recommend to you is probably only possible for mature people who have worked through their issues and conflicts with their parents and relatives. You will not be able to follow this advice if you are still entrapped in enabling or codependent behaviors. *The only way you can really handle all the fuss and bother is to pay for the handfasting yourself.*

This is a hard thing to do. Parents usually have more money, and many have a preconceived notion that they are going to pay for their child's nuptuals. But parents also have an idea that the money they provide allows them to control how it will be spent.

Money is a curious thing. Some parents act as though they have just bought a piece of your soul when they write out the checks for the caterer, the hall, the florist, and so on. Many parents are bullies; some are abusive bullies. They can try to make you believe that you have a responsibility—a holy duty as it were—to make them happy. That you owe it to them to make them happy by doing what they want; by meeting their needs and serving their purposes with your life.

That attitude is psychologically sick and ethically nonsensical. The only people responsible for making your parents happy is your parents, just as your happiness is your responsibility alone. So don't allow them to "buy" control of your ritual, your belief system or your life. If they want to contribute money to the event, make certain that there are no emotional strings attached. Communicate this to them clearly, making sure that they understand that in no way does their contribution allow them to have any say in how it is spent. And make certain that you let them know that if they choose *not* to contribute, your attitude toward them and toward your own beliefs will not change, because the other concept that is difficult to grasp when you are in the grip of planning a hand-fasting is this: Your parents do not "owe" you a wedding. The only people responsible for providing a meaningful and happy ritual and celebration are the couple themselves.

Most parents are willing to freely contribute. A sensible and mature mother when asked for her suggestions—*not her desires*—is usually well-equipped to give good advice. A father who has grown beyond the need to impose his authority on his child is usually only concerned with the love and happiness that the relationship will bring to his child. Parents who have become clear about satisfying their own needs don't care what kind of ritual is held, as long as the "kids are happy." But this excellent state of affairs is available only to people who are willing to communicate openly, be clear and firm on their decisions, refuse to engage in emotional games, and have their spiritual eye on a sacred goal that is far beyond the scope of monotheistic belief systems.

9

RITES OF HANDFASTING

The rituals that follow are examples of ceremonies that are appropriate to Pagans who may be unwilling to invoke large amounts of magickal energies into their lives for any reason. They may be unused to handling energy and either consciously or unconsciously eschew doing a full rite. One of them may be resistant to a Pagan rite (this may mean that the relationship is doomed or will badly warp one or more parties). They may understand that they need to grow and change in order for the relationship to endure. There are many reasons. However, realize that Simple Handfastings are not ineffective and are not some lesser substitute for a "better" ritual. They are exactly what they set out to be: simple, direct, and effective.

Simple Handfastings can serve as rituals of intention. Often when a couple intends to create a High Rite of Handfasting, as is usually the case when both parties are initiated Witches, the couple will make a public statement of their intention and then do magickal work for a given period of time, which leads up to their formal Handfasting.

Simple Handfastings can create a sacred context in which the couple can explore the manifold aspects of their emerging relationship and not the least of those aspects is the possibility that the relationship is not what the individuals need or indeed want. There must always be the opportunity to leave—I heard once of a ritual of intention during which the couple gave each other airplane tickets: single fare one-way flights to distant destinations that were good for several months. I never learned if either of the people took advantage of the opportunity to leave. But the concept is sound: A person cannot choose freely to stay in a relationship if there is no way out of it. It is very like a personal possession: If you can't throw it away, it owns you.

A Simple Handfasting for a Year and a Day

Nina and Collin met at a Pagan gathering, and six months later they decided they wanted to be handfasted. They were both wise enough to know they did not want to commit "for ever and ever."

The following ritual is their Simple Handfasting that can also be used as a ceremony of intention.

Items Used for Ceremony   A low table covered with a pink cloth; a homemade candleholder (made by Collin) with thirteen candles in it, all differently colored (handmade by Nina); a glass of wine; a small decorated spice cake; and a dish containing sea salt and pink and red rose petals.

RITUAL BOOK   The facilitator casts the circle using sea salt and rose petals. No directions are called.

The facilitator speaks:

> We have come together to witness the handfasting for a year and day of Nina and Collin. We add our energies of intention to their energies. We add our good wishes to their good wishes. If there is anyone here who does not agree with this ceremony with their whole heart and soul, they should please leave now.

The facilitator should allow the silence to last about twenty-five heartbeats. (At this point in Nina and Collin's ritual, Collin's brother left.)

The facilitator speaks:

> Now that we are as one on the intention of this ceremony, let us begin. We call here to us the power of the Great Mother, She Who holds all, Who brings all together, and takes all apart. [Pause] We call here the power of the Horned God, He Who protects and He who hunts. Who seeks solutions to the challenges, He who find the ways of passage. [Pause] Nina and Collin, come forward and state your purpose as clearly as you are able.

Nina speaks:

> I am here to be handfasted to Collin for a year and a day, so that we may come to know one another in a space that is magickal and a way that will keep our love alive.

Collin speaks:

> I am here to be handfasted to Nina for a year and a day, that we may be able to enjoy most fully the closeness of our love, discover new ways to be with each other, and to find a place where we can be together forever.

The facilitator speaks:

We have heard you. To those ends we place our energy and our intentions. But all good intentions need an act of binding. Tell us now of your act of binding.

Collin speaks:

I have made this candleholder.

Nina speaks:

I have made these candles.

Both speak:

We hereby agree to meet on the full of each moon for the next year [there were thirteen full moons that year] *and renew our pledges of intention and love. If we should fail to meet, and be it no fault of accident or calamity, then we shall know that this handfasting is not to be.*

All present speak:

We hear you and we witness what you have said.

Collin and Nina then light the first candle; they break the cake and feed each other, and share the pieces around the circle. The facilitator speaks:

Great Mother, Horned Hunter. We thank you for your presence. Let what has been done here—what has been said here—be remembered.

All:

So mote it be.

In the months that followed, Collin and Nina lit four of the candles and then Collin's immaturity and Nina's neediness became obstructive. Nina wanted to start making plans for a "real wedding" and Collin allowed himself to wander into "one nighters," which resulted in bitter fights.

After the fifth and sixth candle had not been lit, the facilitator and the rest of the group along with Nina (but not Collin, since he had refused to attend) took the candles and the candle holder, broke them into many pieces and burned them in an outside fireplace.

Few words were said; the actions were enough. But later some of the older members of the group remarked on how relieved they felt. They also agreed that the first ritual had been a good thing to have done, for it had focused both Nina and Collin on what they were doing in a very real and very magickal way. And although what eventually happened was not what either Nina or Collin felt they wanted, it was surely what needed to happen.

A magickal truth that I will share with you is that magick will give you exactly as much of something as you *need*, but it might be a lot more than you *want*. Keep that in mind when you are planning this very important ritual.

Nina and Collin's example shows clearly one of the uses of a Simple Handfasting or Intention Ceremony. It focuses the people involved on what is really going on and allows for the reality of the situation to surface.

The following example is one of the more successful Simple Handfastings at which I have been the facilitator.

A SIMPLE HANDFASTING FOR A PAGAN AND A MUNDANE

The rite was held in my backyard. Both Celeste and Bob had made special robes for the occasion. Celeste's mother and Bob's parents attended, for although they were not Pagan, all three people realized that their support was important to their children.

ITEMS USED FOR CEREMONY   A picnic table covered in a brightly printed cloth with candles and a bowl of garden flowers on it; small cups of sparkling apple juice (Bob did not drink alcohol); a platter of small decorated cookies; a square of white satin holding two simple gold rings; two small poppets, each made by the couple; an eighteen-inch length of red, white, and green cord made of braided cotton embroidery thread; a small satin pouch; an acorn; a corn kernel; a rosebud; a daisy; a small quartz heart; a small black stone; a feather from a blue jay; a feather from a crow; and a jelly bean and a small piece of foil-wrapped chocolate on a platter in the center of the table.

RITUAL BODY   The facilitator casts the circle:

> *I cast this circle in the name of the Maiden. She who is bright with promise, promising delight. In the name of the Maiden, I cast this circle.*

> *I cast this circle in the name of the Mother. She who is the fertile womb and the nourishing breast. She who brings all to life. In the name of the Mother, I cast this circle.*

> *I cast this circle in the name of the Crone. She who is wise with wisdom, boldly trusting in the dream. In the name of the Crone, I cast this circle.*

> *I cast this circle in the name of the Horned Hunter. He who seeks and finds, He who nurtures and protects. In the name of the Horned Hunter, I cast this circle.*

Celeste's sister calls the East and West directions and a good friend of Bob calls the South and North.

Celeste's sister speaks:

Winds of the East, I call to You that You may come and be here on this day of happiness, that You may guard and protect us and that You may witness the promises made within this rite.

Bob's friend speaks:

Winds of the South, I call to You that You may come and be here on this day of courage, that You may guard and protect us and that You may witness the promises made within this rite.

Sister:

Winds of the West, I call to You that You may come and be here on this day of learning, that You may guard and protect us and that You may witness the promises made within this rite.

Friend:

Winds of the North, I call to You that You may come and be here on this day of oath-taking, that You may guard and protect us and that You may ground and bring into reality the promises made within this rite.

The facilitator speaks:

We are gathered here to witness the handfasting of Celeste and Robert who, after many months of searching and considering, have decided to join their lives together in a ritual of handfasting. They have come to join not only their bodies, but their minds and hearts. Together they will find new ways of resolving the inevitable problems that confront us all. Together they will find the solutions to the obstacles that will attempt to trip them. Let us put forward our energies, our good will, and our love for these people. If there is anyone here who does not feel they can do this, let that person depart now.

(All the participants remained.) The facilitator speaks:

Celeste and Robert, I ask that you step forward and make your intentions known.

Both step forward. Celeste speaks:

I have come here to be handfasted to Robert, because he is the sweetest, kindest, and most honest man I have ever known and ever hope to meet. Robert, you fill my soul with contentment, my mind is challenged by your intelligence, and my whole being made sweet by your presence. I shall love you and care for you and I shall let you teach me with your wisdom and strength.

Bob speaks:

I have come to be handfasted to Celeste, because she is the most honorable and wise woman I have ever met, and because she fills me with a passion that only she can quench. She is a hidden cave of jewels, the source of my serenity, and the fulfillment of my desire. Celeste, I love you now and I shall love you as long as I am able. I shall abide with you, care for you, and allow you to teach and lead me with your kindness and strength.

The facilitator picks up the pouch and, holding it open, presents it to the couple. The facilitator speaks:

Here is the magickal manifestation of your commitment. Choose now what you will put into it; what things will form the substance.

As each item is chosen, it is dropped into the pouch. Celeste speaks:

I choose the feather of the crow, that we may always be able to rid ourselves of that which is dead or outgrown.

Bob speaks:

I choose the acorn, that we may allow something large to grow from something small. That we nurture the promise until it become the reality.

Celeste speaks:

I choose the daisy, because in simple things there is beauty.

Bob speaks:

I choose the rose, for the fragrance of our love is a thing that shall keep us sweet.

Celeste speaks:

I choose the corn kernel, that we may always find sustenance in our love.

Bob speaks:

I choose the heart of crystal, that we may give each other healing.

Celeste speaks:

I choose the stone of reality, that we may face the truth.

Bob speaks:

I choose the blue bird's feather, that we may be assertive and free, never forgetting who we are.

Celeste speaks:

I choose the jelly bean, that we remember to have fun.

Bob speaks:

I choose the chocolate, that our passion remain strong and true.

Celeste and Bob each pick up a poppet. As they hold the poppets together, the facilitator ties the poppets together with the red, white, and green braided thread.

The facilitator speaks:

You have made these promises, you have placed into the realm of magick your wishes and choices. Meditate on this pouch and remember.

The facilitator places the poppets within the pouch and closes it, giving it to Celeste's sister to hold.

The facilitator picks up the rings and says:

These are symbols of love and unity, but they are still individual. Become as one when you face the challenges of the world and the pain that comes with change. But within the union of your handfasting, be your own persons, unique, individual, and always growing. I ask that you allow each other to change, to become more than what you are at present, and that you never find yourself with the bitterness that comes of stagnation.

The facilitator gives the larger ring to Celeste and says:

Celeste, repeat after me the words you yourself have chosen to solemnize your vow: I, Celeste Debroni, do handfast myself to you, Robert Menter, for a year and a day, and for all the future years and days—for as long as our love shall last. I promise to love you and honor you, to care for you in sickness and to support you in times of worry. I will give you my truth while always respecting yours. I am your mate in body, mind, and heart. And to this I give my pledge and the symbol of that pledge, this ring.

Celeste slips ring on Bob's finger. The facilitator speaks:

Robert, repeat after me the words you yourself have chosen to solemnize your vow: I, Robert Menter, do handfast myself to you,

Celeste Debroni, for a year and a day, and for all the future years and days—for as long as our love shall last. I will honor you and respect you, caring for you in sickness and rejoicing with you in happiness. I will hold your uniqueness precious while always valuing my own, and I am your mate in body, mind, and heart. And to this I do give my pledge and the symbol of that pledge, this ring.

Bob slips the ring on Celeste's finger. The facilitator speaks:

Then let us rejoice and feast, that in this place the two have become one, and the circle made fast.

Celeste takes the cookies and feeds one first to Bob, and then shares the cookies with the others saying:

Share with me the sweetness of this day and eat of life, that you may live.

Bob then feeds her a cookie, saying:

Taste the sweetness of our love.

Bob takes the apple juice and first gives Celeste a drink, and then passes the juice out to the others, saying:

Drink of the joy, drink deeply and find your own.

Celeste then gives Bob a drink, saying:

Drink of the strength of our union.

Celeste's sister and Bob's friend then bid farewell to the directions. The say together:

Winds of the East [South, West, North] I bid you thanks and farewell.

The facilitator removes the circle by walking it widdershins while saying:

I take up the wards and windings of power, but let the protection and place of connection remain.

All speak:

So mote it be.

This handfasting provided a very durable foundation for Bob and Celeste's relationship. About eighteen months later, when Bob had a chance to move to the west coast to further his career, Celeste went with him and they had a ceremony with a justice of the peace, which allowed Bob to add Celeste to his insurance coverage. Fourteen years and two children later they are still going strong.

At first glance it may seem as though one of the factors that led to the success of Celeste and Bob's handfasting was that the ritual was more complex, had more energy, and thus more magick put in to the relationship. But both ceremonies were constructed by the participants. Nina and Collin were immature and hasty; rushing in and out of relationships and rituals. They were searching within other people for answers to deep problems that were buried in themselves. Neither really wanted to expend any energy on their relationship; they wanted their partner to do it for them. Celeste and Bob, on the other hand, were willing to put a lot of energy into their handfasting, just as they were willing to put a lot of energy into their relationship.

Nina and Collin were primarily interested in the physical aspects of their relationship, and while Celeste and Bob were also deeply in lust, they realized that the other aspects of a relationship: trust, respect, humor, willingness to change, and so on, were the primary ways to enrich and protect the sex and sensuality that they enjoyed (and still enjoy by all reports) with each other.

Nina and Collin came to their handfasting with unrealistic expectations. In truth, they did not know each other. Their handfasting *served its purpose* in that it allowed them to experience each other in ways that would not have occurred otherwise. The magick of the handfasting allowed them to find out they had little in common except their selfishnesses.

The space that the Rite of Handfasting created in the lives of Nina and Collin is very unlike the space (or purposeful lack thereof) made by a traditional wedding. The space that was created for Celeste and Bob was also much different than that which they would have experienced with a traditional ceremony. They were able to expressly state in powerful and magickal terms that they would stay together as long as the love lasted—not forever. They were also allowed to develop within the context of their relationship the skills and strengths that keep that love alive, rather than bowing to some capricious dicta imposed by deity and society. Nina has since become successfully handfasted to a mature and gentle man that is willing to work on her issues with her. Collin has dropped out of sight. Celeste and Bob have never felt it necessary to re-do their handfasting. The legal ceremony with the justice of the peace was merely expedient.

Sometimes couples come to me requesting a magickal ceremony to cement relationships already joined within a "legal" context. Some were married in Christian churches or Jewish synagogues—often to please and quiet their parents. Some have been "JP'ed" and wanted the spiritual completion of the actions they had started in some judge's chamber. I caution these people to consider very carefully what they are doing.

Often a seemingly stable relationship can crack wide open when the energies of magick are applied to it. This is usually always painful—growth often hurts—and very disruptive. More often than not, it occurs when one of the couple has discovered they are Pagan or have become Witches after the marriage was begun. The desire to have the handfasting is thus unbalanced and the enterprise may well be doomed. But sometimes it is extremely successful.

Alicyn and Rob were such a couple. They had been married for almost five years when Alicyn found her way home to the Craeft. Within a year of her initiation, she became intent on redoing her marriage to Rob.

Rob was a declared agnostic—he had no stated religious or spiritual beliefs, although his strong environmental stance held the Earth to be sacred. While working with Alicyn on her plans to be handfasted, he found that his ideas of what a marriage should be were totally different from hers. They were smart enough to seek professional counseling. The Simple Rite of Handfasting, much like Carol and Mike's, strengthened their relationship—but not without struggle and hard work. The peace and serenity that they have achieved did not come easy, but in Rob's words, "It was worth every tear."

Same-Sex Unions

My experience with homosexual unions is limited, but there is no religious or moral reason why two people who love and respect each other, even though they share the same gender, should not be joined in the rituals of handfasting.

Shari and Nan were two young women from New York City who had moved to southeastern Pennsylvania to distance themselves from Shari's disruptive and abusive parents. They had been in their relationship for five years when they came to me asking if there was some ceremony that I could perform that would make their relationship legal. After I explained the cold and, in my opinion, unconstitutional laws, they went away saddened. About five months later they came back. They had decided that they wanted a ceremony that could be supported by their friends and the more enlightened members of their families. They had also decided to have a child and wanted to bring that child into a supportive family structure. I was able to help them with the writing of their ceremony, but unfortunately, due to an accident was not able to facilitate it. I was, however, able to attend. I found the ceremony moving and the celebration a great deal of fun.

NAN AND SHARI'S RITE OF SIMPLE HANDFASTING

Both women wore white tea-length dresses and both carried flowers. They were attended by Nan's brother and Shari's former roommate. The ceremony was held in a Unitarian church and the reception that followed was at a nearby restaurant managed by a good friend of Nan's.

Nan's brother has a superb voice and he sang an aria as Nan entered from one end of the chamber and Shari entered from the other.

The two women met in the middle of the room, where a small table was set with a candelabrum of colored lights, a glass of white wine, a small chocolate cake, a cup of water, a small stone, and a white ostrich-feather fan.

The facilitator speaks:

I want to welcome everyone who is here tonight to witness the Rite of Handfasting between two of our beloved friends. This ritual is a blessing and confirmation of the steady love and mutual respect that

Nan and Sharon have developed over the past six years. I ask that you take the hands of the people standing next to you and that you join me as we ask for the blessings of the Lady and Lord.

Here in this time and in this place, Great Mother, we ask that You bless us with Your wisdom. That which gives all of us the strength to change and grow and become more of what we are with every passing day. That which gives us the power to achieve what we have the potential to become. With all our hearts, we ask this.

Here in this time and in this place, Lord of Light, we ask that You bless us with Your courage and strength, that we may become ever stronger to deal with the vicissitudes of life, the fear and suspicion of darkened minds, and the eventual struggles that we all must face as we walk Your path. With all our hearts, we ask this.

Nan speaks:

Shari, we have come a long way. From the day we met at the park, we have laughed and cried. We have fought and struggled. We have grown gray hairs and laugh lines. We have grown together. Now, I wish to make our relationship more intense, more complete, and I ask that you join me in that intention. See, I have met you in the middle. Let us go on together until the end.

Shari speaks:

Nan, I have loved your face since the first time I saw it. I didn't want to love you—I wanted to be straight. But with each passing day, with each moon that grew full and then waned, I grew to rely on your humor, to lean on your strengths and to find the means to put up with your spoiled rotten cat. I am ready to join you in making our life more intense, our relationship more complete. See, I have met you in the middle. Let us go on together until the end.

The two women then exchanged the flowers they had been carrying. The facilitator picked up the wine, gave it first to Nan and then to Shari, and said:

Life is sometimes strong and dry. Be prepared.

The facilitator then picked up the chocolate cake and, breaking off a piece, gave it to Shari and then to Nan.

Life is often sweet and moist. Be prepared.

The facilitator then blessed them with the flame of the fire, the sweep of the wind (from the fan), the strength of stone, and the fluidity of water.

Nan and Shari exchanged rings and whispered secret vows to each other, and then as Nan's brother played a waltz on his electric piano, the two danced down the aisle into the foyer of the church.

This was a simple and beautiful handfasting. It did exactly what the two women wanted: It made a strong statement to their community as to their intentions, and it elicited support from friends and family, support that proved so necessary when Nan gave birth to a little boy with congenital heart problems. This story has a happy ending—Nan and Shari are living in California and their son is doing well. Both Shari and Nan have a good relationship with the child's father, who shares custody with them. Although I have not seen them in person for several years, I receive letters twice a year. When I told them that I was writing this book, they both expressed great enthusiasm and said, "Be sure and mention how much the public statement and having a group of friends at the witnessing of an intentional joining can assist people in creating their own personal reality of a relationship." Nan and Shari brought a lot of work and love into being and they founded it on a bedrock of magickal energy and that is one of the primary purposes of handfasting.

The next ritual is the handfasting of an initiate Witch and a Pagan studying to be initiated. It shares some of the main elements as ones previously discussed. The ceremony was held outdoors in a sheep meadow, and the celebration followed in a nearby barn. A small Blessing Fire was lit shortly before the ceremony. A cloth-covered picnic table was the altar, and the candles were in large mason jars. Although the couple used incense, it made little difference in the wind.

HANDFASTING CEREMONY FOR SWANDREAMER AND WHITE TREE

PARTICIPANTS   High Priest (HP), High Priestess (HPS), the Man and Woman to be joined, their witnesses, a Caster, a Summoner, and three women representing the Maiden, Mother, and Crone.

NECESSARY ELEMENTS   A cup of water; a willow wand; a stone; a meter-long cord of braided green, white, and red thread; a loaf of handmade bread; and a goblet of dry red wine.

The altar is decorated with white and red candles and a light floral incense is burning. The ritual cauldron is filled with flowers. The bread and wine are on the altar.

All guests gather within the circle area. The HP and HPS, the couple, and their witnesses stand apart outside of the circle.

The Caster calls the circle and the Summoner calls the quarters. When the HPS gives the signal that all are ready, the

Caster and Summoner open a space through the circle. Holding holly boughs so that they are arching over the magickal gate, the Caster and Summoner allow the wedding party to enter.

The HPS, the Man, and the male witness enter first. There should be a substantial pause.

Then the HP, the female witness, and the Woman enter. It is traditional that the Woman be preceded by a piper or flutist. (In this case we were fortunate enough to have a piper who played the bagpipes.)

The HP and HPS take their places at the altar with the HPS standing to the left of the HP. The Man and his witness take their places and the Woman and her witness take their places, (see diagram).

HPS   [altar]   HP

Man Woman

Witness Witness

The Caster and Summoner close the gate.
The HPS speaks:

Today we are gathered in this space made sacred by the will of those here to witness the Rite of Handfasting. I ask that all of you who stand here to witness do so in high courage and good will. Join, if you can, your hands and your hearts, as I invoke the presence of Goddess.

Goddess! Mother of all. Matrix of all Being, Green Hills of Home! Womb of Birth and Arms of Death and Cauldron of Rebirth. It is to You we call, that You may come and bless this holy rite. Many are the names Your children have called You, secret is Your name within our hearts. Infinite are Your faces and yet Your countenance is never seen. I call to You, hear me! Enter into the space that I have made for You, that You may confirm and bless this fasting of hearts and hands for as long as the love shall last. Lady of Laughter, Love, and Joy, come!

The HP speaks:

I call the One who is the Protector, the One who is the Hunter. He who is the source of wise counsel and consolation. Lord, we ask that You come here now, into the space we have made for You that You may confirm and bless this fasting of hearts and hands for as long as the love shall last. Lord of Passion, Happiness, and Endurance, come!

There is a short pause; then the HP speaks:

We call here one of our own, [Man's name]. Come forward and make your intent known to all assembled here.

The Man speaks first, standing in front of the altar, facing the HPS.

I, [name] do come to stand before you, and all those present to witness that it be known that I intend to be handfasted to [partner's name].

The Woman comes forward, preceded by flower maidens and followed by both legal witnesses. She stands in front of the altar facing the HP. The Woman speaks:

I, [name], do come to stand before you, and all those present to witness that it be known that I intend to be handfasted to [partner's name].

The Man and Woman give the HP and HPS the rings. The HPS holds them up so that all assembled can see them and says:

These are symbols of eternity, the endless round of creation, destruction, and rebirth. I bless them and charge them with the powers of Earth, Air, Fire, and Water, and in Her Names, Maiden, Mother, Crone, and the Unnameable. As the circle is one and yet is made of infinite arcs, so you will be one, and yet express yourselves as infinite individuals. Trust and honor one another with honesty. Love each other enough to let the other grow in his and her own time. Never cease to grow yourself, to dream, and to cast off all that you have outgrown. Her Love is the manifest process of creation and change. You must never say "This is good enough; this must never change," for in stagnation there is corruption and in the still of sameness, decadence. Value each other's newness every waking moment and your love will stay as fresh as this day.

The HP blesses rings in the name of the Horned God, and makes comments he sees fit about marriage.

The Maiden comes forward with a cup of water and pours it out upon the ground, saying:

This is the Water of Life, from which we all have come. It is my gift to you that you may never know the drought of barrenness in body, mind, or spirit.

The Mother comes forward with the willow wand. She gives it to the Woman who then gives it to the Man. She says:

This is the wand of the willow tree; it can bend where others break. My gift to you is the gift of compromise, of bending in the rage of anger, of giving in while in the grip of selfishness.

The Crone comes forward with the stone. She gives it to the Man who then gives it to the Woman. The Crone says,

This is the stone of reality, hard, rigid, and cold. My gift to you is the gift of seeing what is really so, a gift of never being deluded by illusions, and the courage to dream and hope in the face of all.

The HPS addresses the Man:

[Name], repeat after me: [She now reads the vows that the couple have written.]

The Man puts the ring on the Woman's finger.

The HP addresses the Woman:

[Name], repeat after me: [He now reads the vows that the couple have written.]

The Woman puts the ring on the Man's finger.

The HPS reaches across to the Woman and turns back her veil. She says:

[Man's name], look upon the Goddess. For in Her face is the face of every mother and every daughter and every sister that the world shall know. Witnessed by these present in this sacred space, I do charge you, seal you, and bind you, heartjoined and handfast, to abide in affection and honor, for as long as the love shall last.

The HP turns the Man to face the Woman and says to the Woman:

[Woman's name], look upon the God. In him you shall recognize every loving father, every son, and every brother. Witnessed by these present in this sacred space, I do charge you, seal you, and bind you, heartjoined and handfast, to abide in affection and honor, for as long as the love shall last.

At this point the musicians can play a song with meaning to the couple; have the words to the song printed on a sheet of paper so all may join in with the singing.

The HPS and the HP take the braided cord and tie the left hand of the Man to the right hand of the Woman.

The HPS blesses the bread; the HP holds the wine as the HPS blesses it with her athame. They share the bread and wine between themselves.

The HPS hands a piece of the bread to the Woman and says:

> *Eat of the Bread of Life, the gift of the Goddess, that you may taste the sweetness.*

The Woman feeds a piece of the bread to the Man, saying:

> *Taste the sweetness.*

The HP gives the chalice to the Man and says:

> *Drink of the Wine of Immortality. Taste the bitterness of your death and the ecstasy of rebirth.*

The Man gives the Woman a drink, saying:

> *Taste the bitterness and the ecstasy.*

The Summoner and Caster now reopen the gate. The Woman and Man leave the circle followed by the witnesses and the HP and HPS. The guests also follow.

The Blessing Fire should be banked and burning quite low. Any drummer(s) present should start a very fast beat so that the Man and Woman can get a running start to leap the fire. They are followed over the fire by the HP and HPS and all who wish to share in the blessings of the handfasting. The HPS removes the braided cord from the couple's hands and gives it to the Woman. Everyone returns to the circle.

The directional guardians are bade farewell and the circle is released.

10

PREPARATORY RITUALS
FOR THE RITE
OF BECOMING ONE

The Rite of Becoming One is preceded by auxiliary and yet still powerful rituals that serve to focus the participants on the coming transformation of their lives and their magickal shape. Some people hold only one or two of these; others try to meet every month for a rededication ritual. Consider your own time schedule carefully and do not attempt to shove too much into it. In the press to get the elements of the major ritual planned, it is best to hold fewer rituals that are well done than twelve that are scattered and half-formed due to time pressures.

The following is a powerful and yet short ritual that will allow all the participants to get into a magickal space where they can figure out what it is they really want. During this ritual, it is helpful to have drummers present.

ELEMENTAL WORKING RITE TO EVOKE THE DREAMS AND INTENTIONS OF THE COUPLE

The grounding statement of purpose is made by the HP or HPS:

> *We are working tonight to raise energy for creativity and inspiration. We will invoke the powers of Dream and Intention. To do this we will summon from within ourselves each of the four elements of Creation: Water, Fire, Air, and Earth. We will become these elements, celebrating them within our lives and works. We will summon and invoke the God powers of Apollo as Pythios, Snake Singer; Heracles as the Kathandros, Dream Seer; and Lugh Silverhand, Builder of Cities. We will summon and invoke the Goddess powers of Theatys the Sea Mother, who gives birth to tomorrow; Athena as Arachne, she of Weaving and Embroidery; and Bride, the Poet and Singer. And under all, Great Gaia, founder of reality.*

The circle is now cast by saying:

> *We are making a sacred space for dreaming, for chanting, for the shaping and holding of a new reality. Three times I tread this circle, holding the space open, making the shape of our magick firm. Three times I walk the Path of Inspiration. This Circle is Cast! The Place Between the Worlds is Made!*

The Four Quarters are now summoned by saying:

> *We summon the powers of the East, Dreamers of the Morning Mists.*

> *We summon the powers of the South, Singers of the Noon Sun Shining.*

We summon the powers of the West, Dancers of the Evening Breezes.

We summon the powers of the North, Shapers of the Space of Midnight.

The HPS invokes the goddesses by saying:

That Which Is and That Which Is Not—my words make You finite, but never my love. I am your beloved Priestess, [state name] and I call upon you to enter into me, into the space which I have made for you. Lady of all: Isis, Demeter, Freya, Chichicoatl, Astarte, Ma'at, and you Theatys, you Arachne, you Bride! Be here now!

The HP invokes the gods by saying:

I call on You; I say You listen; I say You harken: Pythios, Heracles, Lugh! Come wright me; fashion me as You will. Look through my eyes, speak with my tongue, touch with my hands. EVO-HE!

Next, the statement of ritual purpose is made. The HPS speaks:

God and Goddess, we have called You here to make magick. The magick to dream and intend. The power to find answers and solutions. The strength to carry through with our intentions and plans. We desire the magick of Your Water, Your Fire, Your Air, and Your Earth, and the magick of Your Spirit. Surround us with your rainbow and let us become Your Magicks.

Ground! [pause] Center! [pause] Be Here! [pause] Close your eyes and let your spirit flow out like fingers, let them reach down and out and up and in. Bring those fingers together and intertwine them with one another's spirits. You are reaching deeply and widely, high and handsome.

The HPS pauses for a space of fifty heartbeats. (It is important not to break the building of this tension too soon.)
The HPS speaks:

As you feel the power building within you, allow yourself to hear the surf on the shore. Allow yourself to smell the tang of the sea air. Now—reach out and touch the Sea, feel the Oceans, feel the prophecy. Feel the beginnings, the dreams of possibilities. Dance the dreams, let the waters flow through you and let the water be the colors of the rainbow.

The HPS pauses for a space of fifty heartbeats. On her signal, the drummer(s) should start a slow, muffled, sea rhythm. The participants may dance or drum as their magickal needs dictate.
The HPS speaks:

Now, take the power of the ancient Sea and reach up to the stars and feel the power of Fire, of Will unhindered, of Spirit unfettered. Feel the hot fire of Desire. Be the Fire, sing the words of power.

The HPS again pauses for the space of fifty heartbeats. The beat of the drums should become louder and faster. The HPS should encourage the participants to sing the magick that comes into their mouths. (This may be words that have meaning only to them, or chants that are common to all.)
The HPS speaks:

Use the sea and the fire and allow yourself to touch the four quarters of the windscape. Feel the Air, move with the winds of Growth and Change, let your old ways and methods blow away. Blow with the winds, see inward and outward with the Eye of the Hurricane.

The HPS pauses for fifty heartbeats as the drums become louder and faster. She then signals the drummer(s) to slow the rhythm and lower the sound level.

The HPS speaks:

Reach down into the Earth and feel the shape of reality. Find the perfection of being imperfect. Find the Truth of Chaos, which is the fire within the Gem of Order, the diamond of infinite facets. As you find the fire within the stone, you become the Gems of Her Creation.

The HPS pauses as the drum fades into silence.
The HPS speaks:

Now float with the spirit, float with the tides of time, find the Tree. See the Tree, look at its fruits, find your fruit and eat it. Sink down to the ground, letting all the energy pass through you, into the Tree and back into the earth. As the energy flows listen to the Voice of the Goddess and God. Open your spirit and see Their Shadows. Listen to the drum of Their Power, dance with the Shadow you have summoned.

The drum should return to a normal rhythm, and dancing should commence. Each person should dance with whatever shadow they have summoned. When the dancing and drumming has reached an apogee, crystalize the energy and bring it down.
The HPS speaks:

Now take a piece of the energy and form it into a big crystal bubble and let the bubble go out into the universe, to heal and mend, to bring change and peace into the hearts and minds of all humankind. Keep only what you need to assist you in the coming days to find the answers, solutions and compromises you will need to make. Keep whatever strength and courage you need as you face obstacles and bigotry. Keep good humor and the ability to laugh at yourself. That is the path of sanity.

And now we release the winds of the directions, asking that if they go, they go in peace.

And we release the power of the thrice-cast circle, that it may reside here to catch us if we should stumble and slip, and to hold us in love and comfort when the dark is long and the night bitter. For we have met most merrily, and we shall part most merrily, and merrily, we shall meet again.

All say:

Hey!!

Following this ritual there should a brief session in which all the participants are able to share what they experienced and what they perceived. For the next three or four nights, any dreams should be written down in magickal journals.

Three months before the date of the Rite of Becoming One, the Ritual of Intentional Uniting of Magickal Energies should be held.

This is a simple ritual in which the couple being handfasted give each other magickal jewelry, gear, and sacred objects. Sometimes a Rite of Venus will follow. Again, all dreams and meditations must be written down so that the patterns of energy evolving out of the rituals can be observed and discussed.

The ritual can be done by the two people alone, or in front of their coven, or with only a facilitator and witness present.

All magickal objects are placed on a table that is lit with candles and decorated with flowers. The couple stand facing each other, and they pick up the objects one by one, explain what each object is, what it does for the person, and any history that might be relevant. It is then handed to or placed on the other person. When the process is finished, the couple take each other's hands and, looking directly into each other's eyes, say, *"This is the shape of my soul. Now I wear your shape. I am my magick, now I am you. You are your magick, now you are me."*

If the Rite of Venus is to follow, it should follow immediately, with facilitator and witness leaving the area quickly and discreetly.

The purpose of the Rite of Venus is not only to enter into each other's skins and psyches; it is to also raise energy for the approaching transformation of their lives.

I must insert a caution here, for the Rite of Venus is extremely powerful and in the wrong hands can do magickal damage. This ritual is not about sexual satisfaction and lust, it is about becoming the other person. That means if either one of the couple has unshared secrets, hidden agendas, or abuse triggers, those issues will surface during the ritual and that might blow the relationship apart. On the other hand, that is the exact purpose of the ritual, to learn and share the innermost secrets of the other person. The Rite of Venus cannot be done with either person unwilling, or with any intent to keep some things hidden.

Tina and Matt performed this ritual two months before their handfasting. Matt discovered that he could not hide his bisexuality and Tina found she was unable to accept it. They parted with a great deal of animosity. However, as sad as it was, this way is far more preferable than if Tina had discovered Matt's "secret" *after* the handfasting.

Annie and Will also preformed the Rite of Venus about three months before their handfasting. Annie came to realize that some of her behaviors were triggered by actions by Will that reminded her of her sexually abusive grandfather. Will recognized that his behaviors were mirrors of his alcoholic father. Armed with this information, they were able to work out effective methods of dealing with their triggers and responses.

For both parties, the rite did what it set out to do—to allow the couple to share their innermost feelings and secrets.

Because of conflicts and lack of trust (and perhaps a lack of willingness to accept change) the former had a painful conclusion, but the latter brought about a difficult but successful change.

THE RITE OF VENUS

I want to warn my readers that the following ritual is sexually explicit. My purpose is not to titillate but to elucidate; to speak openly and plainly about sacred sexuality and the barriers that may inhibit it. I will also report only those results that I have actually experienced or that have been shared with me by individuals who understand that I am including their experiences in this book.

The best place to perform this rite is in a luxurious hotel with room service. If that is not available, use a private room where no one from the outside world will intrude, one that has bathroom facilities.

The Rite takes a full twenty-four hours to complete. An even better time budget would be forty-eight, including preparations and regrounding.

Careful preparations are essential, for once the rite begins it is imperative that both people remain within the sacred space. Food and drink, candles, incense, perfume, flowers, special clothing, bath oil, massage oil, tissues, toilet paper, music, towels, sheets, pillows, and so on need to be gathered in the ritual space before the rite commences.

Disconnect the phone if possible. No TV, no radio, no e-mail is allowed. There should be no disturbances from the outside world (unless you call for Champagne and lobster from room service and even then, instruct the bellhop to leave it outside the door).

Make certain that room is warm enough to be comfortable when naked. If it is a bit chilly, silk robes and pajamas lend an air of pampered elegance and will keep you warm without bulk. I suppose this rite could be done with flannel nightgowns but that image is a bit contrary to the sensual aspect of this rite.

When the final preparations have been made, close and lock the door, draw the blinds, and dim the lights.

Using a small table, set out your favorite altar pieces, including an incense burner, candles, any votive figures that are in harmony with the intention of the ritual, a glass of wine (or juice) and a small piece of whole-grain bread. Use only a little incense (a light rose or lily is most appropriate). If you are allergic to incense and perfume, do without, as this rite is about complete comfort, openness, and sharing.

Walk together around the room, blessing the doors and windows that they might be barriers to any energies that are not to your purpose, that only health, sanity, and prosperity may come through them. Bless the drainpipes of the tub, shower, toilet, and sink, as well as the spigots, that the water they allow to enter and that the water they release serve your purposes of magickally enhancing your health, wisdom, and pleasure.

Sit across from one another on the floor, and slowly cast aside your clothing. As each piece is removed, say what barrier to intimacy it is that you are taking off, something like "I remove these shoes, that I may better feel the Earth beneath you." "I remove this shirt that my heart and yours may be closer." You will need to devise your own words, for only your own words and images will be effective. You may want to think about the words ahead of time, and if something spontaneously changes, make notice of it. This is a rite in which the Wise Self often speaks.

When you are naked, light the candles and gaze on the other person, seeing everything about your partner—not just what you want to see. See the midriff bulge, the zit, the mole, the scar, everything that is of that person. Now "see" those same marks, assets, and defects on yourself. Do not envision your own—envision what exists on your beloved, and hold that image.

Now look again, looking *below* the skin to the wrinkles and oddities of personality, to the graces and clumsinesses, and once more, envision them as your own traits, your own strength and weaknesses.

Help each other up and bathe together (or if the tub is too small, shower together). Wash each other carefully, making certain that all orifices are cleaned. Brush each other's teeth and floss. Clean each other's ears and trim each other's toenails. If your partner needs to relieve either bladder or bowels, clean that part afterward with respect and love. If you find you are having difficulty in allowing the person you love and respect most in the world to do these things for you, go back to the altar and seek an answer. Say what comes into your mind without reservation. If you cannot share your innermost thoughts in this scenario, it is unlikely that you will be able to share them in any scenario.

After the cleansing part of the rite, the couple should indulge each other with music, stories, sharing thoughts and dreams. They should feed each other and give each other drink. When you put a piece of food in your partner's mouth, allow yourself to taste and smell what your partner is perceiving; allow yourself to swallow the nourishment of the love you are sharing. As the state of relaxation grows deeper, sexual intimacy should develop with stroking and caresses. Allow yourself to feel the other person's pleasure and, most importantly, consciously allow the other person to enter inside your skin and feel your sensations. If you feel violated or invaded, stop. Talk about what is happening and try to work through any minor conflicts. If difficult feelings persist or become painful, stop the ritual. If you discover that you are trying to manipulate the other person rather than communicate, again, talk about what is happening.

As the sexual tension grows, use your shamanic training to step outside yourself (I call it Left-Shifting) and see yourself as a glowing image inside the body of the other person. Immerse yourself in the otherness of your beloved, and allow it to become self.

Here is an image I have found helpful: Each of us has a silver shamanic cord, which runs out of our navel, that connects us to the world we call real and to our individual lives. Allow yourself to see that cord intertwining with that of your mate, and more importantly, feel your partner's intertwine with *you*. Allow yourself to be with that feeling for several minutes. Allow the other person's strengths and weaknesses to enter you, and match those characteristics with your own weaknesses and strengths.

In addition to the silver navel cord, we all have a multicolored and multifaceted shamanic cord that enters our body right below the left shoulder blade. That cord connects us to the Universe and to Divinity and to the Web of All-Being. Often in our pain and misguided cultural learning, we have taught ourselves to disregard the cord or even to partially disconnect it. In order to do effective shamanic and magickal work, you need to reconnect and become profoundly aware of the cord.

In the Rite of Venus, you allow yourself to experience the input of your beloved's cord into your own being, and your

cord into your beloved's. As this happens, you will immediately experience a subtle yet powerful shift of consciousness.
You may also become aware of other "beings" who are
intensely concerned with your well-being, your safety, and
your relationship. Do not experience any fear or distrust of
these beings, for they are completely benevolent and will not
intrude any further into your consciousness and experience
than you or your partner wish. My experience shows that these
entities are from the plane of Anathean energy, the plane of
pleasure and joy and beauty. These energies can heal almost
any physical and emotional malady, but only if they are used in
full awareness and deliberate application. At this point in the
Rite of Venus, you will be able to use the energies of the Plane
of Anathea and the presence of the benevolent entities to
enhance and empower your sexual pleasure and power.

As you interact with your partner, become aware of his or
her perceptions, and as you approach climax, deliberately
intend that you shall feel your partner's sexual arousal and
orgasm and that your partner shall feel yours.

Keeping in mind that sexual pleasure is a sacred act in and
of itself as long as there is no coercion or manipulation of the
partner involved, and that you are actually creating a healing
magickal energy that can be used not only for your own purposes but for the healing of others and the world, release your
bliss into the Universe, seeing the cords light up and shimmer
with the ecstasy you have just brought into creation.

When you and your partner have reached surfeit, allow
yourself to sleep, eat, and drink. Take another bath, clean each
other, give each other pleasure, all the while discussing the
other person's perceptual experiences and insights. It is helpful
to write down each other's perceptions and then compare

notes a few days later to see if anything new arises or if your perceptions have expanded or changed.

When it is time to complete the rite, feed each other the bread with the intent to nourish each other's soul, body, and magick. Share the wine, appreciating that your time together is limited and thus every minute will count. There can be no wasted hours or days.

Then "unseal" the plumbing, the door, and the windows. Release any excess energy into the world and back into Mother Earth. Open the door and step out. Notice how different everything looks. Now, go find a tree and hug it, long and hard, thanking your Anathean friends for their assistance. I consider it essential to share your experiences (although not a blow-by-blow account by any means) with someone. It makes your experience become more real.

A man who had been sexually abused as a child had a very difficult time allowing his mate to clean him after defecation. He felt as though he was dirty from such an act and that he was sullying his partner. He told me later that it was in that part of the rite that he remembered the acts that his cousins had perpetrated on him, remembering the abuse not just intellectually but emotionally, in a way that he had never before experienced. His partner helped him work through the issue, but it took more than one Rite of Venus before he was able to get through the challenge without hours of crying.

You can see why the rite can be dangerous. If a person were in deep denial of such issues as this man had, it is possible that he or she could project the abuse onto the other person, act out nonsituationally, and further abuse themselves and their mate. If there is any lack of trust, this rite will force it to the surface.

Anne and Jack found they had no problem with the washing and cleansing issue; their issues arose when they were massaging each other. Anne reported that all of a sudden she found she felt guilty receiving pleasure from having her breasts and buttocks stroked and massaged. However, she had no problem massaging Jack. She also reported feeling as though she were in control of the situation when she was giving Jack pleasure and felt out of control when she was receiving it. At one point in the ritual, she went physically numb and found images of being tied up and molested filling her mind, which actually aroused her. Anne and Jack stopped the rite and discussed what had been happening to Anne. Jack admitted that he had sensed a withholding in her before but had put it down to modesty.

Anne is still in therapy but they have successfully completed the rite and are going to be handfasted in the near future.

I will now share a part of my own experience. My husband and I were having painful difficulties in our marriage, compounded by infertility and the growing awareness that he would never have a child. I had two children by a previous marriage and so for me it was not the utter tragedy that it was for him. In order to get into a place where we could heal each other instead of slicing each other open with emotional razor blades, we enacted a rite.

During the rite I had the extreme pleasure of "becoming" a man, of feeling sexual pleasure from a man's perspective. I looked out of a man's eyes into my own female eyes, I felt my body as I had never felt it before, and I became aware of my own discomforts and issues that I had hidden for many years. The result of this transference was a much deeper and better understanding of my husband's emotional needs and challenges. I stopped resisting his pain over being childless and I let him into my own dark shadows. Even today, I can still recall that being a man is much different from being a woman, not better or stronger, just incredibly different. I can still get in touch with the sense of being within and without at the same moment. The union of such identity was and is extremely blissful. Our relationship took a definite turn for the better and continues to grow stronger and more healthy every day.

11

THE RITE
OF BECOMING ONE

This is an extremely complicated and powerful ritual, which should be undertaken by people who know how to summon and hold immense amounts of energy. It is not for the faint of heart, or for someone who wants to do it "big" because "Bigger is Better."

Following a year of preparatory rituals, including perhaps the Rite of Venus, the couple should decide on a day that is not within the Time of Chaos—between Samhain and Imbolg—and not on a waning or dark moon. Beltaine and Litha are both very good holy days on which to hold a Rite of Becoming One.

The guest list can be as enormous as your budget can stand, but everyone invited should be at least Pagan-friendly. Because of the powerful invocative forces of this ritual, any negative or perverse energies present would have a nasty effect—most likely back on the poor person who is sending them and doesn't have a clue in the world that his or her thoughts can affect anything.

Make certain that all of the attendants are Pagan and that the HPS and HP are in complete accord, since their facilitation will have a tremendous impact on the ritual.

All of these factors should be resolved months in advance of the rite, but it is prudent to keep in mind that people change as they confront issues.

The space should be secure and as beautiful as nature allows. I cannot imagine holding this rite in a building, but it may be necessary. Try to make the location as much like a garden as possible.

Preparations for the rite begin months in advance. In addition to the preparations held for a Simple Handfasting and the High Rite of Handfasting, the Rite of Becoming One includes:

- A handwritten vellum scroll stating the magickal names and the magickal date of the handfasting. It should bear the sigils and symbols of all the people involved in the actual rite and will be signed in blood. In an era that is deeply concerned with AIDS and other blood-borne diseases, it is necessary for everyone to be extremely careful and extremely honest. The magickal essence of blood goes deep into the human psyche and it carries a meaning that that no other substance does. Sterile swabs, individual sterile "sharps" (to prick fingers with), alcohol, and Band-Aids are essential.
- A glass (to hold white wine) that will be broken after the rite. The glass does not need to be expensive.

- An empty metal cauldron big enough so that the glass can be broken in it without endangering the participants.
- Two crystal or metal goblets that are for just the couple and reserved for magickal work.
- Fresh flowers—no artificial flowers are permitted on the participants or on the altar. (The entire purpose of the fresh flowers is to remind us that everything—even beautiful things)—fades and decomposes and returns to the Cauldron of Rebirth, that life is short and must be cherished and used completely.
- A sacred cake, made of nuts and whole grains and fruit. This cake should be made several days in advance with complete concentration on its ritual purpose, which is to nourish the bodies, souls, and magick of the couple.
- Candles, that have never been burned before, in glass containers. They should be allowed to burn out completely and may need to do so without anyone in attendance, so have a bucket of water hidden behind the altar.
- Two silver, platinum, or gold rings. They should not include gemstones.
- A willow branch.
- A black rock.
- A cup of sparkling water.
- Candles in containers marking the four directions.
- At least two witnesses other than the HP and HPS.
- Flower petals with which to strew the ground.
- Male and female Summoners, and three women to represent the Maiden, Mother, and Crone.

The ritual begins at dawn, with the couple, the HPS, and HP greeting the new sun.

Each makes a statement concerning their intentions for the day.

The HPS speaks:

Today, in the light and in the dark, I shall stand in the feet of my Mother, and fill my mouth with Her words, and place Her power in my hands. Today, I shall hold the beauty within me.

The bride speaks:

Today, in the light and in the shadow, I shall become one with my beloved; as streams that meet join and become one mighty river, so shall we flow and carry the beauty with us.

The HP speaks:

Today, in the light and in the dark, I shall speak with the power of the Laughing God, I shall place His Fire within my eyes, and grasp His potency with my fingers and my heart. Today I shall share the beauty with all whom I meet.

The groom speaks:

Today, in the light and in the shadow, I shall become one with my beloved. As the winds that blow do not remain apart, as the flames leap together for the sky, as the rocks join in holding us in precious reality, so we will give our beauty to whomever shall ask.

They can then go back to bed if they wish.

The rite begins at sundown, the exact hour set by astronomical measurement—an almanac or a weather channel on the World Wide Web can furnish you with the exact information for your location.

After the guests have gathered, but before the handfasting party enters the space, a man and a woman (not the couple being handfasted) should cast the circle four times, for the Maiden, the Mother, the Crone and the Laughing Lord. The directions should be called in their most benign aspects.

The male and female Summoners cast the circle. They speak together:

We create this sacred space out of the Divine power that we carry within us—a space created by intention and will. A circle cast in the Names of the Triple Goddess and in the Names of the Triple God. A space created to hold and protect all those who stand within. A circle formed of love and trust, in which a new beginning can begin. So this space is created, so this circle is cast.

The Female Summoner faces East and says:

Lady of Love, Lord of Laughter, we call to You, inviting You to join us, to bathe us with Your sacred powers of emotion. You Who bear the hallowed chalice of Holy Water, Blessed Blood, Sacred Wine, hail and welcome!

The Male Summoner faces South and says:

Lord of Courage, Lady of Intuition, we call to You, inviting You to join us, to burn warmly within us blessing us with Your Powers of Strength. You Who dance amidst the flames of creation, You Who are the wand of desire, hail and welcome!

The Female Summoner faces West and says:

Lady of Wisdom, Lord of Knowledge, we call to You, inviting You to join us, to blow through us that we may see clearly, blessing us with your powers of Mind. You Who understand the illusion and Who possess the wisdom to believe in the Dream, hail and welcome!

The Male Summoner faces North and says:

Lord of Justice, Lady of Time, we call to You, inviting You to join us, grounding us in the work we do, blessing us with Your powers of Manifestation. You Who spoke the word of creation, You Who declared the Laws of Creation, hail and welcome!

The Caster, who should be standing in front of the altar, turns to face the guests and says:

I would like to welcome each and every one of you—friends and family—who have joined us this afternoon to witness this sacred ceremony of handfasting. Today we have gathered to make a sacred space in the fabric of time, a space defined by the intent and will of all who are present. Therefore, I ask you to stand with me, holding your hearts and souls high with courage.

The participants now enter as music plays. The HPS will enter the circle leading the groom's party, the groom should be accompanied by his parents if possible; if that is not possible, then by a good friend. As the groom's party reaches the altar, they should stand on the right side and turn to face the guests. The groom will kiss his parents or friend, and as they take their seats or place in the circle, he will stand to the immediate right of the HPS.

After a slight pause, the flower girls will enter the area, strewing the path with flower petals. The HP will then enter, followed by the bride's party. Finally, the bride, accompanied by her parents (or a friend), will enter. Upon entering, the bride's party will stand to the left of the altar, facing the guests. The bride will kiss her parents or friend, they take their seats, and she will stand to the immediate left of the HP.

The HPS speaks:

Goddess! Mother of All, matrix of all being and no-being, Green Hills of Home! Womb of Birth and Gentle Arms of Death and Awesome Cauldron of Rebirth! It is to You that we call, that You may come and bless this holy rite.

Many are the names Your children have called You yet secret is Your name within our hearts. Infinite are Your faces and yet Your countenance has never been seen.

*I call to You, HEAR ME! Enter into this space I have made for
You, that You may bless and confirm this joining of hearts and fas-
tening of hands for as long as the love between these two shall last.*

*Lady of Laughter Love and Joy, I am Your beloved daughter. I
call You up and I call You forth, I summon You down and I entreat
You in. Manifest Yourself as Mother of Life, Creatrix, and Nurturing
Breast. We are your beloved children who have gathered to celebrate
You and this woman and man on this holy day!*

The HPS now touches the Earth and reaches up toward the
sky and says:

*All that unites and gathers together, all that binds and holds fast,
enter this space that I have made for You!*

There is a pause, and the HPS continues:

*Over a hundred years ago, a British poet, A. H. Swinburne, wrote
a long and wordy poem called "Hertha." When I first heard it, I
apprehended that hidden within the many, many, many, words of the
poem, the Goddess was speaking. And as I listened, some of the words
dropped away, and others took their places. I would like to share with
you—with all respect to Mr. Swinburne—the words of the poem as
Goddess spoke them to me.*

I am that which began,
Out of me the years roll
   Out of me, Gods and Man, they are part—
     I am whole.
Gods change and Man and the form of all,
   I am the constant, I am the soul.

Before ever land was
Before ever the sea
Or soft hair of grass

Or fair limb of tree
Or yet the dear flesh-colored fruit of my branches
I was—and your soul was with me.

First life on my sources,
First drifted and swam
Out of me are the forces
That save it, or damn
Out of me came woman
Out of me came man.
Before ever God was, I am what I am.

Oh my children too dutiful to Gods not of me,
Was I not enough beautiful?
Was it hard to be free?
For behold I am with thee
Am in thee and of thee
And never apart.
I flow through thy life with each beat of thy
    heart.
For I am Mother, not maker
Thou wert born and not made.
No mud-pie creator fashioned thee out of
    clay.
And though my children forsake me
Allured, or afraid,
Making prayers to the gods they have fashioned,
I turn not away.
I am here, in the stars and the sea and the earth
In the work of your hands
In the play of your mirth
I have no need of sacrifice,
I desire no prayer

Just be as you are
And my heart leaps within me,
Beholding my children so fair.

After a pause, the HP steps forward and says:

This is an occasion in which the worldly and the divine come together. This is a time when the boundaries between the mundane and the sacred fall down. For this uniting of a man and a woman is not a private act but a public stand taken together before the whole community as witness.

It is the intent of [Craeft name] and [Craeft name] to weave a cord of magick binding and tie a knot of legal and sacred joining, here—today—in this sacred space. A cord that shall hold them together as the winds of fate blow through their days together, a knot that shall tie them in all happenings of their everyday life, happenings both large and small.

And in the weaving of that cord and tying of that knot, [Craeft name] and [Craeft name] will become a new family, joining the spiraling chain of generations that has given us life, and thus given that life meaning.

And in the union of two people, we acknowledge that more than any other rite of passage that we might celebrate, this rite is one in which the God and the Goddess must work together.

And now it is I who call down into this assembly the power and the presence of the Lord of the Dance.

Shining One! You who were the first note the Goddess sang; You who are the balance; You who are the Protector; You who are the Source of Nourishment, whether of body, mind or spirit; You who are the Divine Rejoicer.

Lord, Come now and protect us, come now and nourish us. Celebrate with us the beauty of our bodies and the sacredness of our souls. You who are the Divine Son, the Sacred Lover, the Holy Brother, I call You now, enter this space that we have made for You, that we may know You and find welcome in Your Presence.

There is a pause, then the HPS speaks:

We call here one of our own. [Bride's birth name, Bride's Craeft name], come forward and make your intent known to all assembled here.

The bride steps forward and states clearly so that everyone can hear:

I, [Craeft name, birth name] do come here to be handfasted to [groom's Craeft name].

The HP speaks:

And again, we call here one of our own. [Groom's birth name, groom's Craeft name], come forward and make your intent known to all assembled here.

The groom steps forward and states clearly:

I, [Craeft name, birth name], do come to stand here to be handfasted to [bride's Craeft name].

The HPS speaks:

[Bride's Craeft name, groom's Craeft name], what you come to do here today is not a small thing, not a thing to be taken on or cast aside lightly. The pledges that you make today are but the first sounds of a new eternity opening, the glad cries of a new way of being.

For on this day you will found a new family within the family of humankind. And it is in the shelter of the family that we are born and we grow, we learn and we work, we love and are loved.

A family is not an instance of now, it reaches forward into the spiral of tomorrow to touch and form the future. A family also extends backward into yesterday, and thus the present—where we now stand—and the future to which we are going. Those times are shaped by our ancestors.

Therefore, it is fitting and relevant that at this time we remember those forebears who have—by their loves and their hates—their carings and their indifferences—their presences and absences—by these acts and many more—molded the two of you, and thus will mold this new family which you are becoming.

Let us call into this place and into this time the memories and faces of. . . .

At this point in the ritual, a list of the bride and groom's deceased ancestors can be read, while the bride's mother and the groom's father light memorial candles.

The ring bearer now comes forward and gives the HP the pouch holding the rings. The HP lifts the rings up so that everyone can see them. Then he holds them while the HPS blesses them:

These are symbols of eternity, the endless round of creation, destruction, and rebirth. I bless them with the powers of Earth, Air, Fire, and Water. I consecrate them in Her aspects as Maiden, Mother, and Crone. I declare them sacred in the name of the Unknowable One.

[Craeft name] and [Craeft name], I charge you to hearken: As the circle is one and yet is made of infinite arcs, so you will be as one. And yet you will express yourselves as infinite individuals. Trust and honor each other with honesty. Love each other enough to let the other grow, dream, and change in his and her own time. Love yourselves enough to allow yourself the same, never cease to grow, to seek the

new within yourself, to find new horizons and new stars. Do not hesitate to cast off that which you have outgrown, or no longer need.

Never say, "This moment must last forever. This experience must never change." For nothing is perfect; perfection means stagnation, and in stagnation there is corruption, bigotry, and ignorance.

I charge you: Experience and manifest Her love of you by every action of your life. For Her love is ever-changing and ever-creating change. Therefore, value the newness of each other, assist each other in the process of change, create growth.

The HPS takes the rings and holds them while HP blesses them:

I bless these rings with the powers of the Horned One, God of wood and stream, of horn, hoof, and antler. I charge them with the power of His spirit, His high, leaping courage, and the flashing excitement of His passion. Let the gifts of the High Lord be instilled into these rings.

May the Great God's most gracious blessings go with these two throughout the time of their union and even—so might be their fates— unto death. Let these rings be so blessed and charged that the wearers always have the clarity of sight to see each other as they are, the kindness to be gentle with that knowledge, and the intensity of spirit to love each other all the more!

A musical interlude can be played as the three women step up to the altar. The Maiden takes up the cup of water and speaks:

This is the water of life. It is my gift to you. May you always remember to laugh, play, sing, and dance.

The Maiden sprinkles water on the bride and groom.

The Mother takes up the willow wand and says:

This is the wand of the willow tree. It will bend where others do break. My gift to you is the gift of compromise, of bending while in the rage of anger, of giving while in the grip of selfishness.

The Mother hands the wand to the bride, who hands it to the groom, who gives it to the HP.

The Crone takes up the rock and says:

This is the rock of reality. It is hard, rigid, and cold. My gift to you is that of clear sight, of seeing what is really true and valuing that truth. I give you the gift of never being deluded by illusions and yet have the courage to dream and hope.

The Crone hands the stone to the groom, who hands it to the bride, who gives it to the HPS.

The HP speaks:

Now, we stand ready to witness as this man and woman make their vows.

The HPS speaks:

Now, we stand ready to witness as this woman and this man enter into a sacred union of their own making.

[Groom's Craeft name], repeat after me: [Bride's birth name, bride's Craeft name], as I stand here in the presence of my Goddess and my God, I hereby vow to you that I will respect you and honor you as my mate and as the Goddess within you. I will give you my trust, and I will give you all reason to trust me. I will snuggle and hold you so long as you want, and I will kiss you as much as you will lend me your lips. I will care for you when you are well, and I will care for

you when you are ill. When you are hungry, I will feed you. And when you don't feel like driving, I will. I will stand by and support you in all that you do, whether we are together or separate. I will strive to understand our differences and intelligences so that we can nurture each other's souls. I will make our house a healthy and comfortable home. I will be your friend and share with you my dreams and fears. And I will love you, as you are and as you will be, for as long as the love shall last.

The HP speaks:

[Bride's Craeft name], repeat after me: [Groom's Craeft name, groom's birth name], as I stand here, in the presence of my Goddess and my God, I hereby vow to you that I will respect you and honor you as my mate, and as the God within you. I will give you my trust, and I will give you all reason to trust me. I will snuggle and hold you so long as you want. And I will kiss you as much as you will lend me your lips. I will care for you when you are well, and I will care for you when you are ill. When you are hungry, I will feed you. And when you don't feel like driving, I will. I will stand by and support you in all that you do, whether we are together or separate. I will strive to understand our differences and intelligences so that we can nurture each other's souls. I will make our house a healthy and comfortable home. I will be your friend and share with you my dreams and fears. And I will love you, as you are and as you will be, for as long as the love shall last.

The HPS then turns to the bride, lifts her veil, and places her hand upon the bride's shoulder. She says to the groom:

[Groom's Craeft name], look upon the Goddess! For in this face is the face of every mother, every daughter, and every sister that the world has known or shall know.

Witnessed by these present here in this sacred space, I do charge you to remember the vows you have made, the vows which seal you and bind you, heartjoined and handfast, to abide together in affection and honor for as long as the love shall last.

The HP then turns to the groom and, placing his hand upon the groom's shoulder, addresses the bride:

[Bride's Craeft name], look upon the God. In His face you shall see the face of every father, son, and brother the world has ever known or shall know. Witnessed by these present here in this sacred space, I do charge you to remember the vows you have made, the vows which seal you and bind you, heartjoined and handfast, to abide together in affection and honor for as long as the love shall last.

The HP and HPS take the cord and tie the left hands of the bride and groom together.

The HPS holds the chalice of wine as the HP blesses it with his athame, saying:

As the Blade is to the Man, so is the Cup to the Woman. There is no greater magick than this, a man and a woman joined in love.

The HPS places the chalice on the altar as the HP takes up the plate of special cake. He holds the plate as the HPS blesses the bread with the rod, saying:

As the Earth is to the Woman, so is the Staff to the Man. There is no greater magick than this, a woman and man joined in honor.

The HP and HPS now share the wine and bread.

The HP takes the up the special chalices and, giving one to the groom, says:

This is the wine of life. Drink deeply and feel the warmth of our love.

The groom drinks and then gives the bride a drink, saying:

Taste the bitterness and the ecstasy that is ours.

The HPS takes the bread and, giving it to the bride, says:

This is the bread of life, the fruit of My womb. Taste its sweetness as you savor each bite.

The bride now gives a piece to the groom, saying:

Taste the sweetness that is ours.

The bride and groom now prick their forefingers and let a drop of blood fall into the breakable glass of wine. The bride speaks:

I give you my power, my magick, and my sight, I charge you— keep them safe for me.

The groom speaks:

I give you my power, my magick, and my sight, I charge you— keep them safe for me.

They then drink the water and blood, taking in the essence of each other's magick. Upon emptying the glass, they drop it into the cauldron, letting it break.

The HP makes a closing statement:

In the presence of the Goddess and all the Gods, in the eyes of all present, and in the respect of the world, I bear witness to the vows which this man and this woman have made in my presence.

The HPS presents the bride and groom to the assembly with the following words:

Heartjoined and handfast, I present to you this couple, [bride's birth name] and [groom's birth name and the couple's shared last name]; [bride's Craeft name] and [groom's Craeft name], who shall live as one among you for as long as the love shall last, be it even unto death.

Today, in light and in shadow, we have walked in beauty. Let that beauty go forth to nourish all of the world, bringing harmony and prosperity into the lives of all it touches.

A broom shall be placed in the path of the bride and groom and as they leave, they step over (or jump) it. Everyone leaving the ritual space should step over the broom, as the space will not be un-cast nor the directions released until after the celebration (preferably the next sunrise).

Recessional music may be played, and the order of the recession is the HP, the bride and groom, the flower girls, the maids of honor and groomsmen, the mother and father of the bride, the mother and father of the groom, and the HPS.

12

ROBES OF GLORY

Perhaps nothing about a handfasting is more fun than the clothing. Almost all of us grew up with a vision of a lovely woman wearing a big white gown with a gaggle of men standing around looking and behaving like bemused penguins. That *is* a lovely picture, and one that many people really want to be *part* of, *and* it is an appropriate image for a handfasting—but it is not the *only* image that a Pagan handfasting can have.

Just as masks have important magickal purposes, so does clothing. A handfasting ceremony is an event in which the color, style, material, and the fun of a garment bears deeply on how the energies will form and how they will be held.

Earlier in this book I suggested renting the big white gown, and I still feel that is a very good option for those people who wish to wear one. It can't be denied that the BWG is an extremely expensive item—thousands of dollars can be spent on it! You need to ask yourself if you really want to put that much of your available resources into a piece of clothing.

Many people do! Just because a person is a Pagan doesn't mean that the symbols of their general culture have no meaning. Many brides will buy a wedding gown, either custommade, ready-to-fit (almost all gowns in a bridal shop fit in this category), or off the rack. Give yourself plenty of time to choose a dress, and get the fitting done correctly—and lots and lots of time for the shop to order the wrong dress, misfit the right dress, and go bankrupt on you the week before the ceremony. (The latter actually happened to a woman I know. She had to get a judge to unimpound her wedding dress!)

If you decide not to buy a gown at a bridal shop, you might want to sew one yourself, or hire a costumer to make one. If you decide to do this, you have a multitude of options open to you; colors, materials, and style choices are endless. So go with your dreams.

Color is important to Pagans—most of us associate different colors with different emotions and powers. Almost any color is appropriate for a handfasting except black. Black is the color of the Crone, and it reflects all light energy (which makes it a very good protection color). A handfasting calls many different energies toward the couple and thus black is not a good choice. Also, black is associated with an adolescent "woo-woo" factor, which equates being a Pagan with being powerful, slightly wicked, grown-up, "cool," and isolated. It can lead to wearing far too much eye makeup, so that one resembles a Racoon God-form more than anything else. It is also slightly ridiculous and not magickally effective when worn out of place. A handfasting is not a place for being cool, detached, wicked, or dangerous. On the other hand, if you simply have to have black, put some other colors in with it. Again, do your own thing. My advice is simply my advice, not a divine law.

White is a nice color, although most of us look horrid in stark white. Stark white is a color of mourning in many cultures, and in some countries, the bride changes clothes from a white traditional dress, which indicates her death to her family, into a colorful dress, which signals her birth into her husband's family. Shades of white, cream, ivory, and beige are easier colors to wear and—hint—pastels are even better. But there is no reason not to indulge in vibrant shades or even prints. In fact, there are many *good* reasons to indulge in vibrant shades. If it makes you look good, if it makes you happy, if it fulfills your dream, wear royal blue, crimson, forest green—whatever is magickally most effective for you is what is correct.

Of course, if you don't want to deal with clothing, you can always go skyclad, although it may be somewhat unsettling for any guests who choose to remain clothed. If you do this, be certain that *everyone* knows that the ceremony will be held skyclad, and please be totally naked; no lacy panties to lend a hint of shame should be allowed. (Bug repellent is probably essential if the skyclad ceremony is outside.)

Ethnic costumes can also be appropriate. The partners in a handfasting I attended several years ago were both of Scottish descent, and they wore their families' plaids with pride and flair. Except for the white of the tunics, all the colors were vibrant shades of red, blue, green, and yellow. It was a magnificent ceremony and the haggis was delicious.

I also attended a ceremony in which the families of both couples came from an ancient mountain culture in southeast Asia. Tak and Yeni wore the exquisitely embroidered nuptial costumes of their tribe, the bon monk (a type of Buddhist monk) had no problems with Tak's American Paganism, and the food was out of this world. Yeni latter told me that wearing the traditional garb had been her choice—her mother had wanted the big white gown!

Unless you are a bonafide member of a tribe of indigenous peoples, I suggest you respect the traditions and rites of those cultures and not indulge in "noble savage" costume. Those peoples have paid a heavy price for being who they are and we should all respect their culture and leave it to them. Besides, nobody respects a wannabe.

Clothing for handfastings does not have to be dressy or special; I know of a bride who bought new blue jeans and hand-tucked white linen shirts for herself, her husband, and her party. Everyone supplied his or her own cowboy boots.

But for the great majority of brides and grooms, we want the clothing to be gloriously special and specific to that day— we want the glamour and glitter and the beads and pearls. All of it, the entire banana split! With the whipped cream and maraschino cherry. And I say, go for it! It will make you feel more powerful, more committed, and more intense. It will add immeasurably to the magick.

While authentic clothing from many historical periods often shows up at Pagan handfastings, in many cases it doesn't seem to enhance the situation or the ritual very well. Really authentic costumes should be made of the fabrics used in the historical period and should be sewn using the techniques of the particular era. This means that the materials almost always have to be linen or wool. Dyes should be vegetable dyes— which equates to dull. Prints should be painted on, and most clothing with prints was worn only by the wealthy. In addition, almost nothing you can buy in the trimming department of a fabric store is authentic—have you ever tried to look for linen lace?

Cotton was not widely used until well into the eighteenth century, and silk was only used by the extremely rich. In addition, the real styles were cumbersome and uncomfortable, and usually unwearable for modern people. It seems unfair that a statue or painting can look elegant and graceful in fifteen meters of cloth, but we can't.

Also, Europe is a much milder place than America in terms of extremes of heat and cold. Most of the summer clothing worn in medieval England would cook a bride in June in Pennsylvania. My big suggestion is to go "fantasy"; the dress can be as lavish or simple as your tastes demand, as decorated or plain as you wish, and made out of just about anything, just as long as it says emphatically, "I am beautiful and this is my day!"

The men's clothing should get just as much attention as that of the women. They too should wear the colors that mean the most to them. Reds and greens and blues in strong male hues look gorgeous with lots of lace and gold braid. I have personally dressed six brides, three grooms, and two entire bridal parties. We have created some incredible costumes indeed.

Mary's dress was floor-length white organza silk with whitework Celtic cutouts through which the full light-peach underskirt showed. Her bodice was made of the same light-peach silk with appliques of reembroidered lace beaded with Celtic and Pagan symbols. She wore the green garter of the Witch and a wreath of small peach and white roses atop her veil.

Carol's dress was white cotton (with an ankle-length skirt since we were in a meadow); she wore daisies in her hair and had bare feet.

Kit wore a deep-green velvet caftan over a white silk tunic dress. The caftan had elaborate gold braiding that trimmed the front opening, the sleeves, and the bottom. She wore a green silk hat with a long, trailing, tulle ribbon that wound around the crown and trailed down her back, serving as her veil. Into the tulle she had pinned tiny sprigs of heather, while the hat's brim was decorated with crystal stars and moons. Brian wore a deep-blue caftan over a white silk tunic and white breeches. His caftan had beaded stripes running up the front and around the sleeves. He wore a green hat around which he wrapped holly and oak leaves. His daughter, Angela, wore a deep-pink caftan with an ivory tunic dress underneath and a wreath of roses in her hair.

Chris wore a gold and green silk sleeveless gown that split at about the knee in front and swept into a train in back; she wore magnolia leaves and gardenias in her hair and carried a bouquet of the same. Frank work a gold and red sleeveless sur-coat with a white shirt and black pants. He also wore his sword. The kids (all four) were dressed in smaller versions of the adult costumes.

Nina wore a white velvet gown with a deep-burgundy velvet cloak; she wore holly in her hair and carried a white faux-fur muff. Glenn wore a pierced leather doublet over a white shirt and black breeches and a silver-gray velvet cloak. He wore a wreath of autumn oak leaves with deer antlers on his head. For the ceremony, he rented "armor" which proved to be so heavy and cold, he was grateful to change into his dancing gear.

Kathy wore the big white gown, with subtle green under-tones. The train was seventeen feet long, with beaded embroi-dery covering it and the skirt—Pagan symbols such as a spider web and a crystal spider were tucked in among the embroi-dered roses and stars. Swarovski crystals, three-millimeter

pearls, real gold beads, five kinds of lace, silk ribbon, silk flowers, and I don't know what else went into the dress. We built it
on the foundation of a wedding dress Kathy had bought off
the rack and spent nine months embellishing it. When we
were through and the dress was ready, it didn't look anything
like the one she had bought.

Maddi and Nate wanted a Renaissance wedding. I ended up
sewing twenty-three costumes, including my husband's and my
own. I was grateful that the cats decided they would go as cats.

Maddie's dress was a sea-blue Thai silk with an underskirt of
cloth of gold, on which 4,500 Swarovski crystals, 3,600 real
pearls, and 1,500 Swarovski rhinestones were sewn on 33 yards
of crisscrossed Japanese gold bullion couching braid. Rhinestones decorated the outside of her train and the same pearls
and rhinestones and crystals made a two-inch-wide band that
went around the top of the bodice and sleeves.

Her maids wore rose-gold Thai silk, with open skirts that
showed white cloth and gold damask underskirts. The gowns
were decorated with elaborate corsages of handmade flowers
created from silk ribbons in bold, vibrant jewelbox colors.
They too had crystals and pearls edging their dresses.

The men wore red Thai silk surcoats over white silk lace-
ruffled shirts and black velvet breeches, knee boots, and professional black felt hats with wide brims and ostrich feathers.
Each surcoat had a Celtic emblem couched onto the back.
Nathan also had a groomsmaid, who wore a dress made of the
same red Thai silk over an underskirt of black cloth of gold
damask with Celtic knotwork couched on the bodice and the
front of the underskirt.

Nathan wore a black velvet surcoat with gold lacings and
red jewels set into the back yoke, over a damask-ribbon jupon
that echoed the colors of Maddie's dress. Under that he wore

a white silk shirt with heavy lace collar and cuffs and red jeweled cording, black velvet breeches, knee-high boots, and a red hat with an enormous white feather.

I also made the flower girls' gowns, the gown for the mother of one of the flower girls, the costume for the HP, my own dress, and my husband's costume. It was a great time sewing.

While that handfasting was one of the most elegant and colorful I have ever facilitated, I have also helped with big white gowns that needed just little touches to become Pagan: a crystal pentagram stitched onto the front, some Celtic knotwork along the edge of the sleeves, and so on.

As you can see, your choice of clothing is limited by very little—your pocketbook, the weather, and my prohibition on the color black (and if you really want black . . . oh well . . .). Again, use your magick and see what the reality of your dreams is; go with whatever will make you feel special and powerful and beautiful.

For people who choose to sew, all the major pattern makers in America have brought out lines of medieval, Renaissance and Tudor costumes, Jane Austen–style clothing, as well as the Civil War. And when looking for trim, which can easily be the most expensive component of the costume, search in the home-decorating departments and upholstery shops.

The final robes of glory about which I will write were the tuxedos that Glenn and Barry wore at their handfasting. One was pure white, with white cane and top hat, the other tuxedo was deep violet (and no, I don't know where he found it), with a gold cane and black top hat. They were a lovely couple who could dance a mean tango. I remember them fondly, for their love for each other was a precious thing to behold. Both men died of AIDS within six months of each other.

13

MUSIC SETS
THE STAGE

As every dramatist knows, music during a play is often essential—it serves to indicate changes of emotion and pace, and it intensifies the drama of the climatic moments. Music is also a gift from the Goddess, and as such it should be treated in a sacred way. Any musicians you hire should be "in tune" with the nature of the ceremony. Once, long ago, I experienced the intense discomfort of having the organist walk out when he realized that the ceremony was Pagan. The groom had "conveniently forgotten" to tell him. That ceremony was a bit strange and since then I have always made a point to talk directly to the musicians to insure that they understand the nature of the ceremony.

Now, I have mentioned music many times, but until this point I have not mentioned any particular pieces that I feel are appropriate for Pagan handfastings. Music is such a matter of individual taste that only the couple involved can really decide what is appropriate for them. I am not a musical expert—in fact I have trouble carrying a tune—but I know that music is an essential part of any handfasting ceremony.

Start thinking about your music months in advance, for like the costumes and site, it will provide a fundamental backdrop for your ceremony. Listen to a lot of different music—mostly instrumental pieces. Sting's "Fields of Gold" jumps immediately to mind as does Andy M. Stewart's "Golden, Golden."

It is wise to remember that your handfasting is in great part a dramatic ritual and needs to be staged like one. Prelude music is important because it grounds the guests and the end of the piece signals the beginning of the ceremony. Several short pieces are better than one long piece. A significant pause should occur between the end of the prelude music and the beginning of the ceremony.

The entry march (processional) of the handfasting party needs to be stately and slow, so that the guests can get a good look at the members of the party, everyone can ooh and ahh over the adorable flower girls and boys, and everyone gets a good gasp from the elegance and beauty of the bride. In Pagan handfastings, the groom gets quite a few "Wows!" too. When you choose the processional music, make certain that the piece is slow enough for a half-step march, but does not linger on too long after everyone is at the altar. If you are using a CD player for music, it is easy to practice the piece several times, and whoever is in charge of handling the CD player should not just abruptly cut the music off but slowly turn down the volume knob so that it seems to fade away.

In the middle of the ceremony, there should be a short piece that entertains the audience while everyone "on stage" catches their breath, moves items about, and in general settles down. This pause is almost essential for the Priestess and Priest. A vocal piece works well for this interlude. Remember that outside space does not have the acoustics that an inside room does and your singer may well need an amplifier and microphone.

A professional electronic keyboard works extremely well in handfasting situations, but remember to make certain that it—and any other electrically powered instrument or CD player—is on a waterproof surface, and that all outlets and extension cords are grounded into a GFI and are capable of carrying the electrical load required by the instruments and the sound system. Put the keyboard a good distance away from any speakers to avoid dissonant feedback.

An additional piece of music called a Blessing Song can be sung or played while the Gifts of the Three are given, but be certain that your Maiden, Mother, and Crone can be heard over it—or have it sung after the Gifts are given.

After the vows are completed and the couple has been presented to the guests, a joyful celebration of music is appropriate as the members of the handfasting party leave the ritual area. My all-time favorite is Beethoven's "Ode to Joy." Another exceptional piece is "Fashioned in the Clay" by Elmer Beal Jr. This song works well when sung by the guests if you have someone who can accompany on guitar or organ. It may be difficult to find, so here is the publisher's address: Folk-Legacy Records, Inc., P. O. Box 1148, Sharon, Conn. 06069 (800-836-0901).

A really wonderful resource on the Web is http://wedding musiccentral.com/songlist.htm. This site offers a good CD at a reasonable cost, as well as an interesting and informative book. The book offers a level of expertise that I do not possess and

I freely admit using it when facilitating handfastings. I bought both the CD and the book and have been grateful for them many times.

I have used New-Age music for many handfasting rituals, and two favorites of mine are Calverley's albums *Celtic Mysteries* and *Celtic Mysteries II*. The Celtic Twilight series has many wonderful pieces and Relativity, an Irish group that is no longer together, has two CDs that contain beautiful and moving pieces.

Classical music, as long as it doesn't scream "church," has a treasury of suitable pieces and I know several brides that chose to use Pachelbel's Canon in D for their handfastings.

APPENDIX I: LEGAL ISSUES

A question that often comes up when people contact me is, "Will our handfasting be legal?" *Legal* is a strange description to apply to a spiritual matter, but money talks, and marriage laws are really about protecting money. Who can legally be on an insurance claim, collect social security benefits, take advantage of tax benefits for married people, whose children will inherit, and so on, are all determined by each state.

Therefore, like it or not, many states require that someone who is ordained, licensed, or registered in some way "perform" the ceremony in order for it to be considered legal. All states have provided a non-religious way to get married as well—couples can be legally joined by a justice of the peace or a judge. Whether or not this satisfies the religious requirements of non-mainstream faiths is not considered to be the states' problem.

This is where the prejudice against Pagan and other minority religions rears a very ugly head indeed. Many Pagan groups do not believe in hierarchal structure; they do not have one or two people who are the "powers that be," and who therefore have the "authority" to pass that power on to other people. And, although Wiccans and Witches do have initiation rites, most states do not consider this as "being ordained," since ordination in the states's minds requires attendance at a Christian seminary or rabbinical college.

The following list of the marital laws in the fifty states is provided to aid you in figuring out the legality of handfastings in your state. It is current as of late October 2000. It may change tomorrow, so check with your clerk of courts.

ALABAMA Any licensed minister of the gospel in regular communion with the Christian church or society of which he is a member may perform marriages. Also, marriages may be performed by the pastor of any religious society according to the rules of the religious society. Ministers must provide a certificate of the marriage to the judge of probate within one month after the marriage. For more information, contact the clerk for the judge of probate.

ALASKA The minister, priest, or rabbi of any church or congregation in the state may perform marriages. Ministers must provide marriage certificates to the couple married and report the marriage to the Marriage Commissioner. For more information, contact the Marriage Commissioner.

ARIZONA Any licensed or ordained clergyman may perform marriages. Ministers must record the marriage on the marriage license and return it to the clerk of the Superior Court within twenty days after the marriage. For more information, contact the clerk of the Superior Court.

ARKANSAS Any regularly ordained minister or priest of any religious sect or denomination may perform marriages. Ministers must have their ordination credentials filed by the county clerk who will then issue a certificate to the minister. (Author's note: The state of Arkansas was singularly unhelpful in specifying what was considered ordination credentials.) The marriage license must be completed by the minister and returned to the county clerk within sixty days from the date the license was issued. For more information, contact the county clerk.

CALIFORNIA Any priest, minister, or rabbi of any religious denomination who is of the age of eighteen years or over may perform marriages. Ministers must complete the marriage license and return it to the county clerk within four days after the marriage. For more information, contact the county clerk.

COLORADO Marriages may be performed by any minister. (Author's note: Again, Colorado was unhelpful in defining *minister;* the woman at the Secretary of State's office with whom I spoke said that it was anyone who was ordained. When I asked for the definition of *ordained,* she became flustered and said, "Anyone who is a minister.") Ministers must send a marriage certificate to the county clerk. For more information, contact the county clerk.

CONNECTICUT All ordained or licensed clergymen belonging to this state or any other state may perform marriages as long as they continue in the work of the ministry. The marriage license must be completed by the minister and returned to the city or town clerk. For more information, contact the city or town clerk.

DELAWARE Any ordained minister of the gospel and every minister in charge of a recognized church may perform marriages. Ministers do not need to be licensed to perform marriages but they must report their name and address to the local registrar in the district in which they live. Ministers must keep the marriage license or a copy for at least one year. Also the minister must, within four days, complete and return forms required by the State Board of Health to the clerk of the peace. For more information, contact the clerk of the peace.

FLORIDA All regularly ordained ministers of the gospel in communion with some church may perform marriages. Ministers must complete a certificate of marriage and return it to the office from which it was issued. For more information, contact the county clerk.

GEORGIA   Any minister who is authorized by his or her church may perform marriages. Ministers must complete a certificate of marriage and return it to the ordinary within thirty days after the marriage. For more information, contact the ordinary's clerk at the county courthouse.

HAWAII   Any minister may perform marriages if they are authorized by their church to do so. Ministers must obtain a license from the department of health before performing marriages. Ministers must keep a record of all marriages they perform. Ministers must report all marriages they perform to the department of health. For more information, contact the department of health.

IDAHO   Marriages may be performed by priests or ministers of the gospel of any denomination. Ministers must give a marriage certificate to the bride and groom. Also, the minister must complete the license and a copy of the marriage certificate and return it to the recorder who issued it within thirty days after the marriage. For more information, contact the county recorder.

ILLINOIS   Marriages may be performed by ministers of the gospel in regular standing in the church or society to which they belong. The marriage license and certificate must be completed by the minister and returned to the county clerk within thirty days after the marriage. For more information, contact the county clerk.

INDIANA   Ministers of the gospel and priests of every church throughout the state may perform marriages. Ministers must return the marriage license and a certificate of marriage to the clerk of the circuit court within three months after the marriage. For more information, contact the clerk of the circuit court.

IOWA   Ministers of the gospel who are ordained by their church may perform marriages. The minister must give a certificate of marriage to the bride and groom. Also, the minister must report the marriage to the clerk of the district court within fifteen days after the marriage. For more information, contact the clerk of the district court.

KANSAS   Any ordained clergyman of any religious denomination or society may perform marriages. Ministers are required to file credentials of ordination with the judge of a probate court before performing marriages. Minister must return the marriage license and a certificate of marriage to the probate judge who issued the marriage license within ten days after the marriage. For more information, contact the clerk of the probate court.

KENTUCKY   Marriages may be performed by any minister of the gospel or priest of any denomination with any religious society. Ministers must be licensed before performing marriages. See the local county clerk for a license. Ministers must return the marriage license and marriage certificate to the county clerk within three months after the marriage. It is illegal to solicit marriages. For more information, contact the county clerk.

LOUISIANA   Ministers of the gospel or priests of any denomination in regular communion with any religious society may perform marriages. Ministers must register with the clerk of the district court of the parish or with the health department if in New Orleans. After performing a marriage, the minister must complete a marriage certificate and return it to the clerk of the district court. For more information, contact the clerk of the district court.

MAINE   Ordained ministers of the gospel may perform marriages. Ministers must be licensed by the Secretary of State before performing marriages. Application may be made to the town clerk or treasurer. There is a five-dollar fee. After the marriage, the minister must file a copy of the record of marriage with the town clerk. For more information, contact the town clerk.

MARYLAND   Any minister of the gospel authorized by the rules and customs of their church may perform marriages. Ministers must complete the marriage license and marriage certificate and give one certificate to the couple. Another certificate and the license must be returned to the clerk of the Court of Common Pleas within five days after the marriage. For more information, contact the clerk of the Court of Common Pleas.

MASSACHUSETTS   Ordained ministers of the gospel may perform marriages. Before performing marriages, ministers are required to apply for a certificate from the state. For applications write to: The Commonwealth of Massachusetts, Office of the Secretary, Supervisor, Commissions Division, State House, Boston, Massachusetts 02133. Ministers must file a copy of their ordination certificate and a statement from the church saying that the minister is in good standing. Please let the Office of the Secretary know well in advance if you need a statement from the Commonwealth. Ministers must keep records of all marriages they perform. Also, ministers must return a certificate of the marriage to the town clerk or registrar who issued the marriage license and to the town clerk of the town where the marriage was performed. For more information, contact the town clerk or registrar or write to the Secretary of State.

MICHIGAN   A minister of the gospel who is ordained or authorized by his or her church to perform marriages and who is a pastor of a church in this state, or continues to preach the gospel in this state may perform marriages. Ministers must complete a marriage certificate and give one to the couple. Another marriage certificate must be returned to the county clerk who issued the license within ten days after the marriage. For more information, contact the county clerk.

MINNESOTA   Any licensed or ordained minister of the gospel in regular communion with a religious society may perform marriages. Ministers must file a copy of their credentials of ordination with the clerk of the district court of any county. Ministers must give a copy of the marriage certificate to the bride and groom and also file a certificate with the clerk of the district court in the county which issued the marriage license. For more information, contact the clerk of the district court.

MISSISSIPPI   Any ordained minister of the gospel who is in good standing with his or her church may perform marriages. Ministers must send a certificate of marriage to the clerk who issued the marriage license within three months after the marriage. For more information, contact the clerk of the circuit court.

MISSOURI   Marriages may be performed by any clergyman who is a citizen of the United States and who is in good standing with any church or synagogue in this state. Ministers must keep a record of all marriages they perform. They must give the couple a marriage certificate and must complete the marriage license and return it to the recorder of deeds within ninety days after the marriage license was issued. For more information, contact the recorder of deeds.

MONTANA   Ministers of the gospel of any denomination may perform marriages. Ministers must complete and return a marriage certificate to the clerk of the district court within thirty days after the marriage. Also the minister must provide marriage certificates to the bride and groom upon request. For more information, contact the clerk of the district court.

NEBRASKA   Any ordained clergyman whatsoever, without regard to the sect to which they belong, may perform marriages. Ministers must report marriages they perform to the county judge who issued the marriage license within fifteen days after the marriage. Also the minister must provide marriage certificates to the bride and groom upon request. For more information, contact the county clerk.

NEVADA   Any ordained minister in good standing with his denomination, whose denomination is incorporated or organized or established in the State of Nevada may perform marriages. Ministers are required to complete a complicated procedure to obtain a "certificate of permission" to perform marriages. Among other requirements, the applicant's ministry must be primarily one of service to his congregation or denomination and his performance of marriages must be incidental to such service. Contact the county clerk for applications, and for any questions you may have.

NEW HAMPSHIRE   Marriages may be performed by any ordained minister of the gospel who resides in the state and is in good standing with his church. Ministers not residing in the state may obtain permission to perform a marriage upon application to the Secretary of State. (Author's note: The man with whom I spoke in New Hampshire also had difficulty in telling me whether or not Pagan initiation constituted "ordination." He was under the impression that Pagans did not believe in God and therefore could not be ministers or ordained.) Ministers must send a copy of the marriage certificate to the town clerk. For more information, contact the town clerk.

NEW JERSEY   Every minister of every religion may perform marriages. Ministers must complete a certificate of marriage and return it to the county clerk. For more information, contact the county clerk.

NEW MEXICO   Any ordained clergyman whatsoever, without regard to the sect to which he or she may belong may perform marriages. Ministers must provide the county clerk with a marriage certificate within ninety days after the marriage. For more information, contact the county clerk.

NEW YORK   Marriages may be performed by a clergyman or minister of any religion. However, a 1972 court case said that in order for a marriage to be valid, the minister must have an actual church or at least a stated meeting place for worship or any form of religious observance. Ministers do not have to be licensed except that before performing marriages in New York City, the minister must register his or her name and address in the office of the city clerk of the city of New York. Ministers must complete a marriage certificate and return it to the town or city clerk who issued the marriage license within five days after the marriage. For more information, contact the town or city clerk.

NORTH CAROLINA   Any ordained minister of any faith who is authorized to perform marriages by his church may do so. Ministers must complete the marriage license and return it to the register of deeds who issued it. For more information, contact the register of deeds.

NORTH DAKOTA   Ordained ministers of the gospel and priests of every church may perform marriages. Ministers must file a certificate of marriage with the county judge who issued the license within five days after the marriage. Certificates must also be given to the persons married. For more information, contact the county clerk.

OHIO   Any ordained or licensed minister of any religious society or congregation within this state may perform marriages. Before performing a marriage, ministers must present their ordination credentials to the probate judge of any county. The judge will provide the minister with a license to perform marriages. The minister must then present his license to the probate judge in any county in which he performs a marriage. Ministers must send a certificate of marriage to the probate judge of the county that issued the marriage license within thirty days after the marriage. For more information, contact the clerk of the probate court.

OKLAHOMA   Ordained ministers of the gospel of any denomination who are at least eighteen years of age may perform marriages. Ministers must file a copy of their credentials with the county clerk before performing marriages. Ministers must complete a certificate of marriage and return it to the clerk or judge who issued the marriage license. For more information, contact the clerk of the county court.

OREGON   Ministers of any church organized, carrying on its work, and having congregations in this state may perform marriages in this state if authorized by their church to do so. Before performing marriages, ministers must file their credentials with the county clerk of the county in which they reside or in which the marriage is to be performed. Ministers must give the bride and groom a marriage certificate upon request. Also, the minister must send a marriage certificate to the county clerk who issued the marriage license within one month after the marriage. For more information, contact the county clerk.

PENNSYLVANIA   Ministers of any regularly established church or congregation may perform marriages. *Also, persons may marry themselves if they obtain a certificate from the clerk of the orphans' court.* (Emphasis author's.) Ministers must provide a certificate of marriage to the bride and groom. Also, they must send a marriage certificate to the clerk of the orphans' court who issued the marriage license within ten days after the marriage. For more information, contact the clerk of the orphans' court.

RHODE ISLAND   Everyone who has been, or is, the minister of any society professing to meet for religious purposes, or incorporated for the promotion of such purposes, and holding stated and regular services, and who has been ordained according the customs and usages of such society may perform marriages. Ministers must obtain a license from the city or town clerk before performing marriages. Ministers must endorse and return the marriage license to the town or city clerk in which the marriage was performed. For more information, contact the town or city clerk.

SOUTH CAROLINA   Ministers of the gospel who are authorized to administer oaths in this state may perform marriages. Ministers must complete the marriage license and give one copy to the parties and the other two copies must be returned to the county judge of probate who issued it within five days after the marriage. For more information, contact the county judge of probate or his clerk.

SOUTH DAKOTA   Marriages may be performed by a minister of the gospel, or priest of any denomination. Ministers must provide the bride and groom with marriage certificates upon request. Ministers must also keep a record book of all marriages they perform. Finally, the minister must send a marriage certificate to the clerk who issued the marriage license within thirty days after the marriage. For more information, contact the clerk of courts.

TENNESSEE   All regular ministers of the gospel of every denomination, and Jewish rabbis, more than eighteen years of age, having the care of souls may perform marriages. Ministers must endorse the marriage license and return it to the clerk of the county court within three days after the marriage. For more information, contact the county clerk.

TEXAS   Ordained Christian ministers and priests, Jewish rabbis, and persons who are officers of religious organizations and who are duly authorized by the organization to conduct marriage ceremonies may perform marriages. Ministers must complete the marriage license and return it to the county clerk who issued it within thirty days after the marriage. For more information, contact the county clerk.

UTAH   Ministers of the gospel or priests of any denomination who are in regular communion with any religious society may perform marriages. Ministers must provide a certificate of marriage to the county clerk who issued the marriage license within thirty days after the marriage. For more information, contact the county clerk.

VERMONT   Ordained ministers residing in this state may perform marriages. Nonresident ordained ministers may perform marriages with the permission of probate court of the district within which the marriage is to take place. Ministers must complete the marriage license and certificate of marriage and return it to the clerk's office from which it was issued within ten days from the date of the marriage. For more information, contact the town clerk.

VIRGINIA   Ministers of any religious denomination may perform marriages. Before performing marriages, ministers must provide proof of their ordination and proof that they are in regular communion with their church to the circuit court of any county or city or to the corporation court of any city in this state. The judge will then authorize the minister to perform marriages provided the minister obtains a bond in the amount of five hundred dollars. Ministers may receive a fee of no more than ten dollars for performing a marriage. Ministers must complete the marriage certificate and return it to the clerk who issued the marriage license within five days after the marriage. For more information, contact the clerk of the county circuit court or the clerk of the corporation court.

VIRGIN ISLANDS   Clergymen or ministers of any religion, whether they reside in the Virgin Islands or elsewhere in the United States may perform marriages. Ministers must complete the marriage license and return it to the clerk of the municipal court that issued the license within ten days after the marriage is performed. For more information, contact the clerk of the municipal court.

WASHINGTON   Regularly licensed or ordained ministers or any priest of any church or religious denomination anywhere within the state may perform marriages. Ministers must send two certificates of marriage to the county auditor within thirty days after the marriage. For more information, contact the county auditor.

WASHINGTON, D.C.   Ordained ministers of the gospel may perform marriages. Marriage licenses are addressed to the minister who will perform the ceremony. The minister must complete a marriage certificate for the bride and for the groom and return another certificate to the clerk of the District of Columbia Court of General Sessions within ten days after the ceremony. For more information, contact the clerk of the Court of General Sessions.

WEST VIRGINIA   Any minister, priest, or rabbi, over the age of eighteen years, may perform marriages. Before performing marriages, ministers must provide proof of their ordination to the clerk of any county court. The clerk will then provide the minister with an order authorizing them to perform marriages. Ministers must return the completed marriage license to the county clerk who issued it on or before the fifth day of the month following the marriage. For more information, contact the clerk of the county court.

WISCONSIN   Any ordained clergyman of any religious denomination or society may perform marriages. Before performing marriages, ministers must file their credentials of ordination with the clerk of the circuit court in the county in which their church is located. The clerk will give the minister a certificate. Ministers must complete the marriage certificates and give one to the bride and one to the groom. The original must be returned to the registrar of deeds of the county in which the marriage was performed or if performed in a city, to the city health officer. This must be done within three days after the marriage. For more information, contact the clerk of the circuit court.

WYOMING   Every licensed or ordained minister of the gospel may perform marriages. Ministers must give a marriage certificate to the bride and groom upon request and must return a certificate to the county clerk. For more information, contact the county clerk.

As you can see, the laws favor the established mainstream churches and more than one clerk of courts could not give me a definition for the meaning of *ordination* in his particular state. In some cases the reasoning was a paradox: A person was ordained if he was given such authority by his church, and his authority rested on ordination.

Even in liberal states such as Rhode Island, the final decision can be left to the clerk of courts. The only state which seems to recognize individuals' rights to marry themselves is Pennsylvania.

It is essential that anyone facilitating a Pagan handfasting keep records (*permanently*), send the certificate or license in on time, and maintain that he or she is only facilitating the hand-fasting, not in fact performing any religious act of binding— which you and I know is spiritually impossible, but the mainstream hasn't yet heard the news.

In addition, the facilitator should furnish the handfasting couple with his or her own Wiccan or Craeft rola. In addition, I would recommend that the facilitator not utter the words "I pronounce you man and wife" in any handfasting ritual. I also suggest that any facilitator not charge a fee, although the individual should be reimbursed for his or her time and effort as the couple sees fit. Personally, I never charge a fee, only asking that my out-of-pocket expenses be paid.

While I loathe authoritarian hierarchy, it is easy to see why some sort of agreement would be useful in the Pagan community if only to establish a common basis of what the definition of clergy is and what constitutes ordination. Perhaps someday the Witch Wars will die down enough that we will be able to do that.

For now, the Universal Light Church offers free ordination. Visit their site at http://ulc.org/ulchq/discourse1.htm or write to them at ULC, 601 Third St., Modesto, CA 95351 and ask to be ordained. Be certain to read the entire posting or informa-tion packet carefully. Make certain you agree spiritually with what they are saying. Remember that if you receive an ordi-nation through them, they are resting on your credibility as well as you resting on theirs. The site and the organization is well worth researching.

APPENDIX II: INFORMATION SHEETS AND INVITATIONS

The following is an example of an information sheet that I have found useful to hand out to guests. It helps explain what we are and what we are doing, and lets them know that Paganism and WitchCraeft are real, legitimate, and substantial lifestyles and religions.

Welcome to Nathan's and Madelaine's Handfasting

We would like to extend a warm welcome to all the guests, and provide some of you with a brief explanation of the ritual.

Most of you have never attended a Pagan ritual before—almost none of you have been included in the magickal workings of a coven of Witches. Therefore, some of you may find the energy of this ritual unsettling. Some may find it exhilarating. We hope that no one will find it boring.

We are Witches.

We claim that title proudly, in honor of the sacrifices that were made by people who were called Witches—men and women who were persecuted and murdered by the Christian church. The conversion of the Pagan peoples of Europe by the Christian church was one of the bloodiest episodes in the past two thousand years. The Pagan peoples of Europe who refused to convert were almost entirely eliminated during one of the first genocides in all of history, the so-called Conversion of the Barbarians.

For this afternoon, we ask that you set aside all the Hollywood spooky images, all the propaganda, all the hate stories told about Witches. We ask that you open your spirits and mind to a different way, an ancient and yet ever new way of relating to the Earth, to the Universe, and to each other.

We are polytheists.

We worship Divinity in all of the infinite forms that It takes—male and female; old and young, gentle and fierce. We do not worship any evil god, be he called Satan, the Devil, or Beelzebub. Those beliefs belong to the Judeo-Christian-Islamic belief system and have never been a part of ours. And we do not believe in the supreme authority of a transcendent God. Our Gods are immanent and available for us to know personally. Our Gods do not place themselves above justice, morals, or ethical behavior. Our Gods do not demand obedience or submission. We do not need to be saved for we have never been damned and we do not need to be redeemed for we have never been slaves in either mind or spirit.

In this ritual, we will create a sacred space and call to the aspects of Divinity that manifest Themselves as the Directional Guardians and the ancient Elements of Water, Fire, Air, and Earth. We will invoke the Aspect of the Mother Goddess, and the God as Hunter. We will stand witness as Nathan and Madelaine make their vows and marry each other.

Madelaine will not throw her bouquet, instead her maids will throw their floral crowns and anyone who catches one will receive the gift of prosperity in the coming year. No one will smash food into anyone's face, for ours is a belief of nurturing and caring, not one of humiliation and domination. We do not throw rice or birdseed and

Nathan and Madelaine are not required to leave their party just when it is getting to be fun.

If you have any questions, please feel free to ask questions of those of us in costume.

Thank you for coming, and Blessed Be. . . .

The following is an example of an invitation to a handfasting. The magickal names of the two people marrying each other were used in addition to their mundane names. Self-addressed and stamped RSVP cards were enclosed, as was a card with three phone numbers and an e-mail address. A map showing how to get to the location was also tucked into the envelope.

❀ Meris-Kenit ❀
Madelaine Sauk
and
❀ Dioskios ❀
Nathan Kingsbury
request the honor of your presence
at their
Rite of High Handfasting
on
Saturday June third,
Two thousand one C.E.
at
Four o'clock P.M.
The ritual and celebration will take place at
the MotherChant Covenstead
located at
the Meadow in Greensbury

INDEX

Index